"The epistles of 2 Peter and Jude are
book shines a floodlight on their rich
organization, careful exegesis, interact
focus. Harmon offers explanations that a
or obscure. Whether in church or classroom, this book is an excellent summary of the harrowing yet hope-filled message of these short epistles written by firsthand observers of their main subject: Jesus."

Robert W. Yarbrough, Professor of New Testament, Covenant Theological Seminary

"Set in the broader theological context of Scripture, Matthew Harmon usefully summarizes the main theological contributions of these neglected letters. He outlines the considerable theological overlap in the books at the same time as he highlights the distinctive emphases of each letter."

Douglas J. Moo, Kenneth T. Wessner Professor of Biblical Studies, Wheaton College

"Matthew Harmon has written a carefully organized biblical-theological exposition of 2 Peter and Jude from his conservative evangelical perspective."

Peter Davids, Chaplain, Our Lady of Guadalupe Priory; author, *A Theology of James, Peter, and Jude*

"Matthew Harmon's treatment of Jude and 2 Peter balances rich biblical-theological connections with pastoral wisdom and insight and helps readers understand how these two short letters at the end of the New Testament fit within the Bible's great story of redemption. His work will help Christians reengage these important letters to the great benefit of the church!"

Darian Lockett, Professor of New Testament, Talbot School of Theology, Biola University

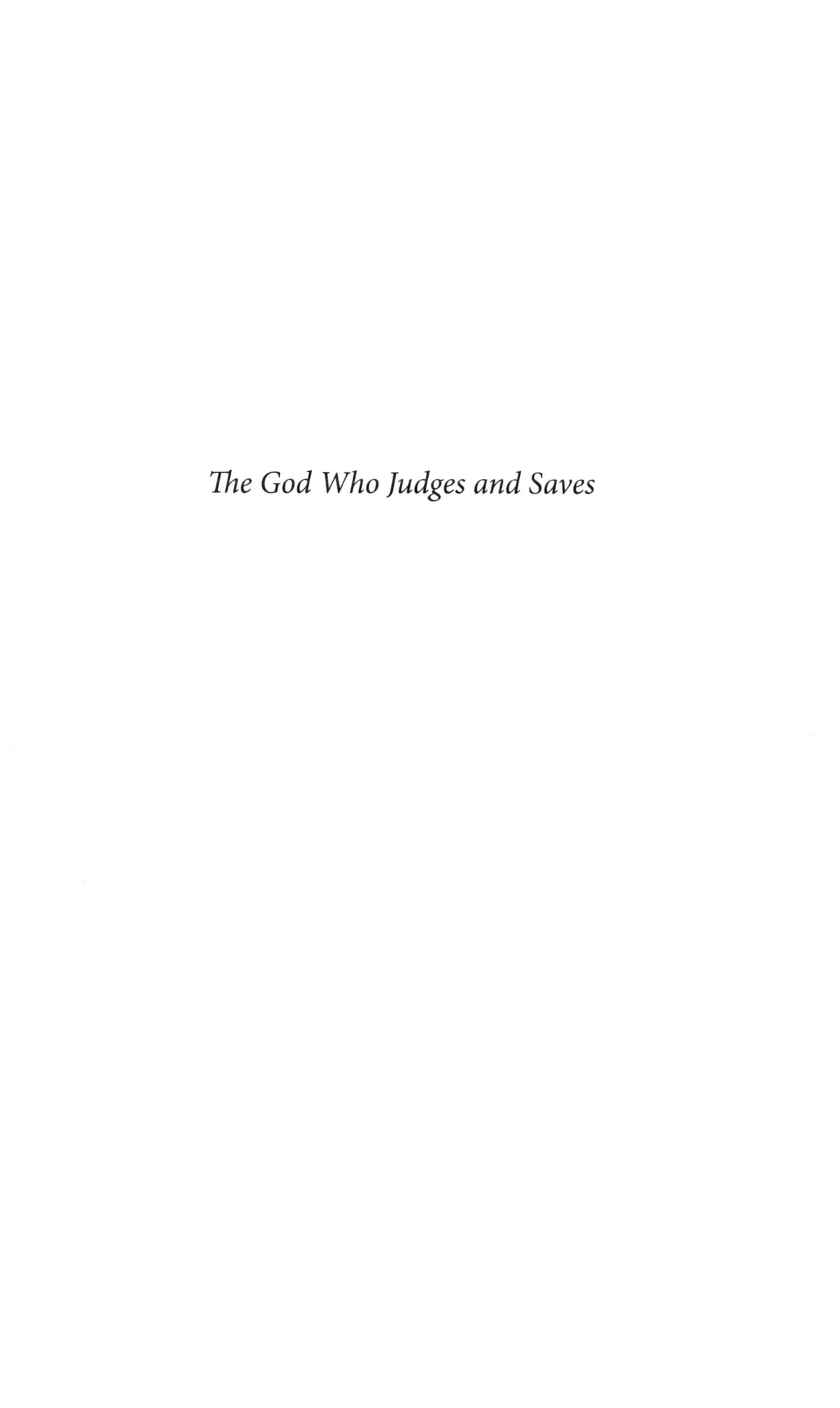

The God Who Judges and Saves

New Testament Theology

Edited by Thomas R. Schreiner and Brian S. Rosner

The Beginning of the Gospel: A Theology of Mark, Peter Orr

From the Manger to the Throne: A Theology of Luke, Benjamin L. Gladd

The Mission of the Triune God: A Theology of Acts, Patrick Schreiner

United to Christ, Walking in the Spirit: A Theology of Ephesians, Benjamin L. Merkle

The God Who Judges and Saves: A Theology of 2 Peter and Jude, Matthew S. Harmon

The Joy of Hearing: A Theology of the Book of Revelation, Thomas R. Schreiner

The God Who Judges and Saves

A Theology of 2 Peter and Jude

Matthew S. Harmon

WHEATON, ILLINOIS

The God Who Judges and Saves: A Theology of 2 Peter and Jude

Published by Crossway
1300 Crescent Street
Wheaton, Illinois 60187

Cover design: Kevin Lipp

First printing 2023

Printed in the United States of America

Scripture quotations marked AT are the author's translation.

All emphases in Scripture quotations have been added by the author.

Trade paperback ISBN: 978-1-4335-7565-5
ePub ISBN: 978-1-4335-7568-6
PDF ISBN: 978-1-4335-7566-2

Library of Congress Cataloging-in-Publication Data

Names: Harmon, Matthew S., author.
Title: The God who judges and saves : a theology of 2 Peter and Jude / Matthew S. Harmon.
Description: Wheaton, Illinois : Crossway, 2023. | Series: New Testament theology | Includes bibliographical references and index.
Identifiers: LCCN 2022014608 (print) | LCCN 2022014609 (ebook) | ISBN 9781433575655 (trade paperback) | ISBN 9781433575662 (pdf) | ISBN 9781433575679 (epub)
Subjects: LCSH: Bible. Peter, 2nd—Theology. | Bible. Jude—Theology.
Classification: LCC BS2795.52 .H37 2023 (print) | LCC BS2795.52 (ebook) | DDC 227/.93—dc23/eng/20220914 LC record available at https://lccn.loc.gov/2022014608 LC ebook record available at https://lccn.loc.gov/2022014609

Crossway is a publishing ministry of Good News Publishers.

VP 33 32 31 30 29 28 27 26 25 24 23
13 12 11 10 9 8 7 6 5 4 3 2 1

To Jesus Christ, who alone deserves glory, majesty, dominion, and authority, before all time and now and forever.

Contents

Series Preface

THERE ARE REMARKABLY FEW TREATMENTS of the big ideas of single books of the New Testament. Readers can find brief coverage in Bible dictionaries, in some commentaries, and in New Testament theologies, but such books are filled with other information and are not devoted to unpacking the theology of each New Testament book in its own right. Technical works concentrating on various themes of New Testament theology often have a narrow focus, treating some aspect of the teaching of, say, Matthew or Hebrews in isolation from the rest of the book's theology.

The New Testament Theology series seeks to fill this gap by providing students of Scripture with readable book-length treatments of the distinctive teaching of each New Testament book or collection of books. The volumes approach the text from the perspective of biblical theology. They pay due attention to the historical and literary dimensions of the text, but their main focus is on presenting the teaching of particular New Testament books about God and his relations to the world on their own terms, maintaining sight of the Bible's overarching narrative and Christocentric focus. Such biblical theology is of fundamental importance to biblical and expository preaching and informs exegesis, systematic theology, and Christian ethics.

The twenty volumes in the series supply comprehensive, scholarly, and accessible treatments of theological themes from an evangelical perspective. We envision them being of value to students, preachers, and interested laypeople. When preparing an expository sermon series, for example, pastors can find a healthy supply of informative commentaries, but there are few options for coming to terms with the overall teaching of each book of the New Testament. As well as being useful in sermon and Bible study preparation, the volumes will also be of value as textbooks in college and seminary exegesis classes. Our prayer is that they contribute to a deeper understanding of and commitment to the kingdom and glory of God in Christ.

Matthew Harmon's volume, *The God Who Judges and Saves,* looks at two of the most neglected books in the Bible, namely, 2 Peter and Jude. Despite their brevity and unenviable location near the end of the canon, Harmon demonstrates the remarkably comprehensive teaching that the two letters contain and its uncanny contemporary relevance. From the inspiration and sufficiency of Scripture to the history of redemption and coming day of the Lord, 2 Peter and Jude offer a full and fresh exposition of the good news of the gospel of the Lord Jesus Christ. Harmon also shows how this theology, with its attention to false teaching and judgment, perseverance and obedience, is a clarion call to living faithfully as a follower of Jesus in our day.

Acknowledgments

GOD HAS USED MANY CIRCUMSTANCES, people, and institutions to make it possible for me to write this book. While the majority of Christians around the world have limited access to advanced theological education, in his providence God has allowed me to study with and learn from a number of faithful scholars who love Jesus, his word, his people, and his world. As a professor at Grace College and Theological Seminary, I have the privilege of interacting with students who are eager to grow in their walk with God by seeing the beauty of Christ in and through Scripture. I am also thankful for an administration that values my writing ministry and provides me with a reduced teaching load to facilitate that.

I am also grateful to God for Tom Schreiner and Brian Rosner inviting me to write this volume. For many years I have admired and benefitted from their scholarship, so being asked by them to contribute to this series is a tremendous honor. Having the opportunity to write another book for Crossway is also a great privilege. Regardless of their role in taking a book from the idea stage to the finished product you are now reading, their love for God overflows into a pursuit of excellence that is contagious.

But when it comes to the people who are most supportive of me in my writing ministry, my family surpasses them all. Watching my two sons, Jon and Jake, grow into godly young men is not only a delight, but a motivation to write books that help them and others better understand the Bible so they can know God better and follow Jesus more closely. However, when it comes to the person who is most enthusiastic and supportive of me and my writing ministry, no one surpasses my wife, Kate. To borrow words from Jonathan Edwards, God has given us an "uncommon union" that is "of such a nature, as I trust is spiritual, and therefore will continue forever."[1] Kate, you are my greatest earthly treasure and I marvel at God's kindness to me through you.

1 Jonathan Edwards, *Correspondence by, to, and about Edwards and His Family*, vol. 32, *The Works of Jonathan Edwards Online*, Jonathan Edwards Center at Yale University, accessed March 31, 2022, http://edwards.yale.edu/.

Abbreviations

Agr.	*De agricultura*
Ant.	*Jewish Antiquities*
Apoc. Ab.	*Apocalypse of Abraham*
Apoc. Mos.	*Apocalypse of Moses*
BDAG	*Greek-English Lexicon of the New Testament and Other Early Christian Literature*, 3rd ed.
BECNT	Baker Exegetical Commentary on the New Testament
BTNT	Biblical Theology of the New Testament
ConBNT	Coniectanea neotestamentica or Coniectanea biblica: New Testament Series
EEC	Evangelical Exegetical Commentary Series
1 En.	*1 Enoch* (*Ethiopoc Apocalypse*)
JSNT	*Journal for the Study of the New Testament*
Jub.	*Jubilees*
L.A.B.	*Liber antiquitatum biblicarum*
Leg.	*Legum allegoriae*
NIVAC	NIV Application Commentary
NSBT	New Studies in Biblical Theology
NTS	*New Testament Studies*
Num. Rab.	*Numbers Rabbah*
Plant.	*De plantation*
PNTC	Pillar New Testament Commentary
Sobr.	*De sobrietate*

Spec.	*De specialibus legibus* (Philo)
T. Benj.	*Testament of Benjamin*
T. Levi	*Testament of Levi*
TDNT	*Theological Dictionary of the New Testament*
Tg. Ps.-J.	*Targum Pseudo-Jonathan*
WBC	Word Biblical Commentary

Introduction

IF YOU WERE TO ASK CHRISTIANS to name their favorite books of the Bible, it is unlikely that 2 Peter or Jude would make the top of many lists. They are short letters, tucked away toward the back of the New Testament. In contrast to the four Gospels and Paul's letters, many believers rarely read, let alone study, these two letters. Jude and 2 Peter also contain content that strikes many contemporary readers as strange, even referring to events and writings not found in the Old Testament. As a result, many Bible readers conclude that 2 Peter and Jude are best treated like a distant relative that one sees occasionally but never goes out of the way to spend any significant time getting to know.

But as contemporary Christians we neglect 2 Peter and Jude to our own peril. Despite being almost two thousand years removed from when Peter and Jude wrote these letters, the contemporary church faces many of the same challenges. Critics from both inside and outside the church question the authority, inspiration, and inerrancy of Scripture. Christians are condemned as judgmental for believing that God will one day render judgment on those who persist in their disobedience to him. False teachers openly question God's word and twist it for their own selfish gain, seeking to lead others away from the true gospel through lives of immorality. Those who seek to be faithful to Jesus find themselves under constant pressure from the surrounding culture to abandon "the faith that was once for all delivered to the saints" (Jude 3). Scoffers dismiss as a naïve fairy tale our belief that one day Jesus will indeed return for his people and usher in a new heavens and a new earth. Understood this way, the church today has much to learn from 2 Peter and Jude about how to live faithfully as followers of Jesus.

The starting point for seeing how 2 Peter and Jude help us faithfully follow Jesus today is to first understand (to the best of our ability) the historical situations that Peter and Jude address when writing. To that end we should briefly summarize what I have discussed at further length in my work in the ESV Expository Commentary series.[1]

Despite questions about its authenticity, 2 Peter was written by "Simeon Peter, a servant and apostle of Jesus Christ" (1:1). As a key leader in the early church, Peter preached the gospel throughout the Roman Empire, including Corinth (1 Cor. 1:12) and Syrian Antioch (Gal. 2:11) among others. Facing an imminent death at the hands of Nero sometime in the mid-60s (2 Pet. 1:12–15), Peter writes to an unspecified group of Christians (though perhaps the same recipients as 1 Peter; see 2 Pet. 3:1) to leave them a tangible reminder of the truth of the gospel and call them to pursue growth in godliness as they await Christ's return and the arrival of the new heavens and new earth. Standing in their way are false teachers who deny Jesus Christ as their Lord and Master through their immoral lives (2:4–22) and dismissive scoffing at the promise of Christ's return (3:1–13).

The epistle of Jude has also faced questions about its authenticity throughout the history of the church. But a strong case can be made that the author is Jude the half-brother of Jesus (Matt. 13:55), even though he simply identifies himself as "Jude, a servant of Jesus Christ and brother of James" (Jude 1). Although Jude appears to be writing to a specific church or group of churches, he does not specify who they are. Given the fact that Jude expects his audience to be familiar with Jewish apocryphal literature/traditions, his audience is likely Jewish believers (though one should not rule out a mixed congregation of Jews and Gentiles). These believers (perhaps living in a Gentile city somewhere in Palestine) had been infiltrated by false teachers who promoted their

1 Matthew S. Harmon, "2 Peter," in *Hebrews–Revelation*, ed. Iain M. Duguid, James M. Hamilton, and Jay Sklar, vol. 12, ESV Expository Commentary (Wheaton, IL: Crossway, 2018), 363–410; and Matthew S. Harmon, "Jude," in *Hebrews–Revelation*, 503–24.

own authority on dreams while at the same time rejecting the authority of God, and perhaps church leaders as well (8, 11–13). Because they rejected God's authority, they indulged in sexual immorality and were motivated by greed (7–8, 11–13). These actions produced division in the church and led to vulnerable members within the church being led astray (16, 19, 22–23).

Based on that foundation, we can identify the theological concepts that the author articulates as well as the underlying theological convictions that inform what the author says. Although written by two different men, 2 Peter and Jude can be discussed together in light of the extensive overlap of shared material in the two letters. But we must be careful that this shared material not distract us from the different emphases in each letter. Although a theology of 1 Peter is treated in a separate volume in the series, from time to time we will draw in material from 1 Peter to help shed light on 2 Peter when helpful.

Each chapter of this book identifies a key theme that is present in both 2 Peter and Jude. Inevitably, because many of the themes discussed are tightly interconnected, there will be some measure of unavoidable repetition at points. While I have attempted to explain how each theme is developed within 2 Peter and Jude, an important element of biblical theology is to set that theme within the scope of the rest of Scripture. Both Peter and Jude were men whose worldview and conceptual frameworks were profoundly shaped by previous Scripture. In that sense, this book shares a similar approach to that of James Hamilton, who defines biblical theology as "the interpretive perspective reflected in the way the biblical authors have presented their understanding of earlier Scripture, redemptive history, and the events they are describing, recounting, celebrating, or addressing in narratives, poems, proverbs, letters, and apocalypses."[2] He goes on to explain why this task is so important. "Our aim is to trace out the contours of the network of assumptions reflected in the writings of the biblical authors. If we can

2 James M. Hamilton, *What Is Biblical Theology? A Guide to the Bible's Story, Symbolism, and Patterns* (Wheaton, IL: Crossway, 2014), 16.

see what the biblical authors assumed about story, symbol, and church, we will glimpse the world as they saw it. *To catch a glimpse of the world as they saw it is to see the real world.*"[3]

That then is the goal of this short book on the theology of 2 Peter and Jude—to catch a glimpse of the world as they saw it so that we today can see the world as it really is. With that in mind, why not take a moment to pray for God to open your eyes to see wondrous things from his word (Ps. 119:18)?

3 Hamilton, *What Is Biblical Theology?*, 19; emphasis added.

1

The Word of God

THE BIBLE FROM BEGINNING TO END shows us that God is a speaking God. Indeed, Genesis 1 emphasizes that God creates by speaking, with each of the six days beginning with the expression "And God said" (Gen. 1:3, 6, 9, 14, 20, 24). Revelation concludes with the risen Jesus announcing, "Surely I am coming soon" (Rev. 22:20). In between these two biblical bookends (seemingly on almost every page!) the Bible recounts God speaking in some shape or form.

Yet alongside this pervasive theme of God speaking is an important related theme that runs from the beginning to the end of the Bible: the enemies of God seek to undermine or dismiss God's word. The very first words of the serpent when attempting to deceive Eve were "Did God actually say?" (Gen. 3:1). As the final step before ushering in the new heavens and the new earth, God casts the devil, who deceived humanity, into the lake of fire, along with all who rejected the truth of God's word (Rev. 20:10, 15; 21:6–8). In the entire period between Eden and the new Eden God's enemies actively seek to discredit or dismiss the word of God.

Against that backdrop, it should not surprise us that in our own day there are many who seek to undermine the truthfulness and reliability of God's word.[1] Both Peter and Jude faced opponents who in some

1 For a helpful resource that responds to a wide range of contemporary challenges to Scripture, see D. A. Carson, *The Enduring Authority of the Christian Scriptures* (Grand Rapids, MI: Eerdmans, 2016).

fashion attacked the word of God, and rather than back down in fear Peter and Jude enthusiastically defended Scripture from a variety of different angles. More than that, they unapologetically used Scripture to make and illustrate their points.

To help us organize what 2 Peter and Jude tell us about God's word, we will approach the subject under three separate (but related) headings. First, we will explore how Scripture is sufficient for life and godliness. Second, we will examine how Scripture is both a human and a divine product. Third, we will explain the nascent twofold structure of Scripture. And before concluding the chapter, we will look briefly at what books were considered Scripture.

Scripture as Sufficient for Life and Godliness

The sufficiency of God's word for life and godliness has its roots in the garden of Eden. Following the pattern of Genesis 1, God speaks humanity into existence:

> Then God said, "Let us make man in our image, after our likeness. And let them have dominion over the fish of the sea and over the birds of the heavens and over the livestock and over all the earth and over every creeping thing that creeps on the earth." So God created man in his own image, in the image of God he created him; male and female he created them. (Gen. 1:26–27)

As part of blessing humanity, God not only commissions them but provides for their ongoing sustenance by announcing, "Behold, I have given you every plant yielding seed that is on the face of all the earth, and every tree with seed in its fruit. You shall have them for food" (Gen. 1:29).

Genesis 2 further reveals that God's word is the source of both life and godliness. After placing the man in the garden "to work it and keep it" (Gen. 2:15)—thus consecrating him as a priest[2]—God issues a command:

2 On Adam's priestly role, see Andrew S. Malone, *God's Mediators: A Biblical Theology of Priesthood*, NSBT 43 (Downers Grove, IL: InterVarsity Press, 2017), 47–57.

> And the LORD God commanded the man, saying, "You may surely eat of every tree of the garden, but of the tree of the knowledge of good and evil you shall not eat, for in the day that you eat of it you shall surely die." (Gen. 2:16–17)

By obeying God's word—one might even say by being godly—humanity would continue to experience life in God's presence and avoid the death that comes from disobedience.

Of course, Adam and Eve disobeyed God's command with catastrophic results (Gen. 3:1–24). Their disobedience led to judgment (Gen. 3:14–24) and spiritual death (Rom. 5:12–14). In particular, Adam and Eve were barred from Eden so that they could not "take also of the tree of life and eat, and live forever" (Gen. 3:22), with God going so far as placing "cherubim and a flaming sword that turned every way to guard the way to the tree of life" (Gen. 3:24). Yet embedded within the words of judgment were also words of promise that gave them life and hope. An offspring of the woman would one day crush the head of the serpent (Gen. 3:15). Instead of immediately ending their physical lives, God slaughtered an animal to provide Adam and Eve with garments of skin (Gen. 3:21). Adam and Eve were made spiritually alive by their faith in these promises.

A similar pattern is present in Deuteronomy, where Moses prepares a new generation of Israelites to inherit the promised land. Recalling Israel's encounter with God at Mount Sinai, Moses explains that on that day God instructed him, "Gather the people to me, that I may let them hear my words, so that they may learn to fear me all the days that they live on the earth, and that they may teach their children so" (Deut. 4:10). Fearing Yahweh is at the heart of godliness, and that fear was the appropriate response to hearing, trusting, and living in obedience to God's word. A primary reason that God fed Israel with manna for forty years in the wilderness was "that he might make you know that man does not live by bread alone, but man lives by every word that comes from the mouth of the LORD" (Deut. 8:3).

At the conclusion of his life, Moses issues this stern warning to Israel:

> Take to heart all the words by which I am warning you today, that you may command them to your children, that they may be careful to do all the words of this law. For it is no empty word for you, but your very life, and by this word you shall live long in the land that you are going over the Jordan to possess. (Deut. 32:46–47)

Note again the twin themes of life and godliness in connection with God's word. The words that God speaks are the source of life for Israel, and living in obedience to them is an expression of godliness.

The sufficiency of God's word for life and godliness is a prominent theme in the Wisdom Literature as well. Perhaps the preeminent example of this is found in Psalm 119. Twice the psalmist explicitly prays "give me life according to your word!" (Ps. 119:25, 107; cf. 119:37, 40, 50, 88, 93, 116, 144, 149, 154, 156). By living according to God's word one can be blameless (Ps. 119:1, 80), unashamed (Ps. 119:6, 31, 116), upright (Ps. 119:7), pure (Ps. 119:9), steadfast/faithful (Ps. 119:5, 30), and wise (Ps. 119:66, 98–100, 125, 144, 169). Especially noteworthy is the number of verses that connect God's promises with life, such as verse 50: "This is my comfort in my affliction, that your promise gives me life" (cf. 119:116, 154).

It is against this backdrop that we must understand Peter's claim in 2 Peter 1:3–4:

> His divine power has granted to us all things that pertain to life and godliness, through the knowledge of him who called us to his own glory and excellence, by which he has granted to us his precious and very great promises, so that through them you may become partakers of the divine nature, having escaped from the corruption that is in the world because of sinful desire.

God has given everything necessary for people to experience spiritual life through the word of the Lord announced in the gospel (1 Pet. 1:22–2:3). It is through the proclamation of God's word that people are "born again to a living hope" (1 Pet. 1:3), and it is God's word that sustains the spiritual life of believers until they enter "into the eternal kingdom of our Lord and Savior Jesus Christ" (2 Pet. 1:11).

The promises found in God's word are also sufficient for godliness, a term that describes a life that is single-mindedly oriented toward God and is expressed in one's thoughts, feelings, desires, actions, and words. Godliness captures the essence of what Jesus referred to as the greatest commandment: "You shall love the Lord your God with all your heart and with all your soul and with all your mind" (Matt. 22:37, citing Deut. 6:5). Everything that a person needs to live a godly life comes through God's word and in particular through "his precious and very great promises." It is through these promises that believers "become partakers of the divine nature," an expression that refers to the restoration of the image of God that had been corrupted and distorted when Adam rebelled (2 Pet. 1:4).

On this basis, Peter calls believers to pursue a series of virtues that work out in practical ways the promises found in God's word (2 Pet. 1:5–7). The ongoing growth of these virtues leads to an effective and fruitful life (1:8), imagery that may even recall God's original commission of Adam to "be fruitful and multiply and fill the earth" (Gen. 1:28). Believers experience this effective and fruitful life by "the knowledge of our Lord Jesus Christ" (2 Pet. 1:8), which is, of course, mediated through God's word. From the firm foundation of forgiveness of sins and ongoing growth in godliness experienced through God's powerful word, believers can diligently confirm their calling and election and, in doing so, ensure their entrance into Christ's eternal kingdom on the last day (1:10–11). Through the written word of God believers have a perpetual reminder of what God has already done for them through Christ, what he is currently doing in them by his Spirit, and what he promises to do for them on the last day (1:12–15). Shortly after reminding believers to remember God's word communicated through "the predictions of the apostles of our Lord Jesus Christ" (Jude 17), Jude pronounces this blessing over his readers:

> Now to him who is able to keep you from stumbling and to present you blameless before the presence of his glory with great joy, to

> the only God, our Savior, through Jesus Christ our Lord, be glory, majesty, dominion, and authority, before all time and now and forever. Amen. (24–25)

There should be little doubt that one of the primary ways that God is able to prevent believers from stumbling and present them before himself blameless is through the word of God.

As believers live in this fallen and hostile world as sojourners and exiles (1 Pet. 2:11–12), they can expect to face mockery from scoffers. In response to their mocking question, "Where is the promise of his coming?" and their claims that nothing has changed since "the beginning of creation" (2 Pet. 3:4), Peter reminds his readers of five key truths from Scripture. First, God formed the earth out of water through the word of God (3:5), an allusion to Genesis 1:9–10. Second, it was also through water and God's word that the world was deluged as an act of judgment (an allusion to Gen. 6–8), and by that same word the current heavens and earth are being preserved for judgment (2 Pet. 3:7). Third, the Lord is not slow in keeping his promises, since "with the Lord one day is as a thousand years, and a thousand years as one day" (3:8, alluding to Ps. 90:4). Fourth, Peter reminds his readers that "the day of the Lord will come like a thief" (2 Pet. 3:10), language that echoes the teaching of Jesus in Matthew 24:43. Finally, after calling believers to a life of holiness in anticipation of the last day (3:11–12), Peter writes that "according to his promise we are waiting for new heavens and a new earth in which righteousness dwells" (3:13). The apostle borrows ideas and language from several texts in Isaiah (e.g., Isa. 32:16; 43:16–21; 51:3; 60:21; 65:17–25; 66:22) to remind believers of God's promises of a new creation where he will dwell with his people. Scripture is sufficient to strengthen believers even in the face of taunts from scoffers.

A final example of Peter and Jude's belief in the sufficiency of Scripture is their extended use of scriptural examples as a paradigm to help their readers evaluate the false teachers they are facing. Indeed, it is in this regard that Jude and 2 Peter show their most significant overlap. They bring forth the examples of Cain (Jude 11), angelic disobedience (2 Pet. 2:4; Jude 6), the flood (2 Pet. 2:5), Sodom and Gomorrah (2 Pet. 2:6; Jude 7), Lot (2 Pet. 2:7–8), the exodus (Jude 5), Korah's rebellion (Jude 11), and Balaam (2 Pet. 2:15–16; Jude 11). As 2 Peter 2:9 summarizes, they use these scriptural examples to show that "the Lord knows how to rescue the godly from trials, and to keep the unrighteous under punishment until the day of judgment." The scriptural examples help their readers to see that the false teachers are just the latest version of a pattern that runs throughout redemptive history. By trusting in what God has said through "the predictions of the holy prophets and the commandment of the Lord and Savior through your apostles," believers have all that they need to stand firm in the face of scoffers and false teachers (2 Pet. 3:1–13). In doing so they will be able "to contend for the faith that was once for all delivered to the saints" (Jude 3) and keep themselves in the love of God as they await Christ's return (17–23).

From start to finish and every point in between, Scripture is sufficient for the spiritual life and growth in godliness of God's people.

Scripture as a Powerful Human and Divine Word

Scripture is both a human and a divine product. In 2 Peter and Jude we see both of these realities expressed, though the emphasis falls on Scripture as a divine word. But in presenting Scripture as a human and divine product, both Peter and Jude are simply extending what earlier Scripture claimed for itself.

A good place to start is 2 Peter 1:19–21. He intends his letter to serve as a reminder of the truths of the gospel long after his death (1:12–15). Likely drawing on the Old Testament precedent of a judicial proceeding requiring the testimony of two or more witnesses (Deut. 19:15), Peter offers two witnesses to the truthfulness of the gospel. The first is the eyewitness testimony of the apostles (2 Pet. 1:16–18), using the particular example of the transfiguration (cf. Matt. 17:1–8; Mark 9:2–8; Luke 9:28–36). The second witness is the word of God (2 Pet. 1:19–21). What he writes is so important that we will quote it in full:

> And we have the prophetic word more fully confirmed, to which you will do well to pay attention as to a lamp shining in a dark place, until the day dawns and the morning star rises in your hearts, knowing this first of all, that no prophecy of Scripture comes from someone's own interpretation. For no prophecy was ever produced by the will of man, but men spoke from God as they were carried along by the Holy Spirit.

These verses have much to say about both the human and divine aspects of Scripture. Let's focus on three particular insights.

First, Scripture is a prophetic word. In the most basic sense, a prophet is someone who receives what God says and speaks or writes those words to others. The Old Testament portrays Moses as the paradigmatic prophet.[3] When Moses protests God's commission to lead Israel out of Egypt on the basis of being "slow of speech and of tongue" (Ex. 4:10), Yahweh responds by reminding him that he is the one who not only made Moses's mouth but will also "be with your mouth and teach you what you shall speak" (Ex. 4:12). Israel is so terrified upon hearing God speak the Ten Commandments directly to them from Mount Sinai that they say to Moses, "You speak to us, and we will listen; but do not let God speak to us, lest we die" (Ex. 20:19). At the close of his life, Moses announces that "the LORD your God will raise up for you a prophet like me from among you, from your brothers—it is to him you shall listen. . . . And I will put my words in his mouth, and he shall speak to them all that I command him" (Deut. 18:15, 18). This basic pattern of God placing his words in the mouth of the prophet to enable him to speak those words to his people regularly appears in accounts where God commissions a prophet (e.g., Jer. 1:4–12; Ezek. 3:1–11).

3 Although Gen. 1–2 does not explicitly say so, Adam is portrayed as a prophet in that he receives God's word (Gen. 2:16–17) and presumably passes it on to Eve, who knows what God said to Adam (Gen. 3:2–3); see further Benjamin L. Gladd, *From Adam and Israel to the Church: A Biblical Theology of the People of God* (Downers Grove, IL: IVP Academic, 2019), 18–19.

In referring to the prophetic word, Peter has in view the entire Old Testament, though perhaps with a particular emphasis on the network of Old Testament texts alluded to and echoed in Peter's description of the transfiguration (2 Pet. 1:16–18).[4] Referring to God the Father as the "Majestic Glory" likely echoes the assertion in Psalm 8:2 that Yahweh's majesty is above the heavens. Designating Jesus as the "beloved Son" draws on a network of texts such as Genesis 22:2, 12, 16 (where Isaac is referred to as Abraham's beloved son); 2 Samuel 7:14 (where God promises to be a father to David's promised offspring); Psalm 2:7 (where Yahweh addresses his anointed as his Son); and Isaiah 42:1 (where Yahweh refers to his chosen servant as his beloved). In saying that he was on the "holy mountain" with Jesus, Peter may be echoing Psalm 2:6, where Yahweh announces that he has set his anointed king "on Zion, my holy hill." Each of these texts was a prophetic word spoken by God through human authors, who sometimes did not fully grasp the meaning and significance of what God was saying through them (1 Pet. 1:10–12).

Second, the truthfulness and reliability of Scripture has been consistently confirmed. The experience of Peter, James, and John at the transfiguration is just one example of God demonstrating that his word is trustworthy. Peter then uses additional Old Testament language to portray the reliability of God's word (2 Pet. 1:19). Describing it as "a lamp shining in a dark place" picks up language from several psalms that associate God's word with light or lamps (Pss. 19:8; 119:105, 130). In the Old Testament the dawning of the day can be a general metaphor for God providing comfort (Pss. 27:6; 46:5; 130:6) or a more specific picture of the arrival of God's eschatological acts (Isa. 9:2; Mal. 4:2). The reference to the "morning star" picks up the promise of a royal deliverer who would defeat the enemies of God's people (Num. 24:14–19). Because these promises, patterns, and pictures of the Messiah in the

4 Philo uses similar expressions to refer to the entire OT (e.g., *Leg.* 3.43; *Plant.* 1.117; *Sobr.* 1.68). For more on the suggested OT allusions and echoes that follow, see further Matthew S. Harmon, "2 Peter," in *Hebrews–Revelation*, ed. Iain M. Duguid, James M. Hamilton, and Jay Sklar, vol. 12, ESV Expository Commentary (Wheaton, IL: Crossway, 2018), 380–82.

Old Testament have been fulfilled with the arrival of Christ, believers can have an unshakable confidence in God's word and trust him to fulfill what has not yet come to pass.

Third, God is the source of Scripture, while man is its conduit. Peter places side by side the human and divine roles in producing Scripture. God's role can be summarized under two categories. First, he is the source of Scripture. That is likely what Peter means when he writes that "no prophecy of Scripture comes from someone's own interpretation" (2 Pet. 1:20).[5] The Bible does not originate in the creativity or brilliance of human authors. God speaking is the origin of Scripture; had he remained silent, there would be no Bible. Second, through the Holy Spirit God is the one who empowered human beings to speak. Like the wind that fills the sail of a ship and enables it to move forward, God's Spirit enabled human beings to speak what God inspired them to say and write.[6]

Although not stated explicitly, the human role in the production of Scripture can be reasonably inferred from what Peter does say. Simply put, the human authors had to surrender themselves to following the prompting of God through his Spirit. The starting point for Scripture is not the decision of the human author to write (i.e., "the will of man"), but rather the prior action of God to reveal himself through that human author.[7] In order to hear what God was saying, the human authors of Scripture adopted the kind

5 The underlying Greek expression is difficult. Another possibility is that this expression means that prophecy cannot be interpreted according to the whims of the interpreter. But the surrounding context as well as the use of similar expressions in Jewish literature to defend the divine origins of OT prophecy favor the view presented here; see further Harmon, "2 Peter," 383.

6 Peter uses language that is similar to how both Josephus (*Ant.* 4.119) and Philo (*Spec.* 1.65) describe God working in the prophets to move them to speak for him.

7 Scripture notes multiple ways that God worked in the human authors to produce authoritative Scripture. Sometimes he spoke audibly and instructed the author to write down exactly what he said (e.g., Jer. 30:2; Rev. 19:9). But more often God prompted the human author to record what God was doing along with its meaning and significance. Yet even in these situations God is the source of Scripture through his act of taking the initiative to prompt the human author to write.

of humble posture described in Isaiah 66:2—"But this is the one to whom I will look: he who is humble and contrite in spirit and trembles at my word." The Holy Spirit may have been the wind that filled the sail, but the sail had to be properly positioned in order for the wind to fill it.

Peter returns to the power of God's word when he addresses those who mock the promise of Christ's return. They must remember what God has said through the apostles and the prophets (2 Pet. 3:1–3). When such mockers question the promise of Christ's return, they deliberately ignore the fact that God created the world, judged it through the flood, and currently preserves it until the day of judgment by his word (3:5–7). In contrast to these mockers who deliberately overlook what Scripture clearly teaches, believers should call to mind several truths rooted in what Scripture says. Peter borrows language from Psalm 90:4 to remind believers that "with the Lord one day is as a thousand years, and a thousand years as one day" (2 Pet. 3:8). An echo of Habakkuk 2:3 supports Peter's claim that the Lord is not slow to fulfill his promises; he is simply providing more time for sinners to repent (2 Pet. 3:9). The sudden arrival of the day of the Lord like a thief in the night mirrors Jesus's own teaching (Matt. 24:43), while the destruction of the current creation finds expression in several Old Testament texts (e.g., Isa. 24:19; 34:4; Mic. 1:4; Nah. 1:5). By living lives of godliness in anticipation of the day of the Lord, believers are actually "hastening the coming of the day of God" (2 Pet. 3:12, echoing Isa. 60:22). Drawing language and imagery from several texts in Isaiah (e.g., 32:16; 43:16–21; 51:3; 60:21; 65:17–25; 66:2), Peter reminds believers that we are "waiting for new heavens and a new earth in which righteousness dwells" (2 Pet. 3:13).

Given that Scripture is a powerful divine word, written down by the human authors, and reliable and trustworthy, it is no wonder that God's people are reminded that "you will do well to pay attention" to it (1:19). Believers should adopt a posture of constant readiness to hear, believe, and apply what God's word says since it is in fact sufficient for all things pertaining to life and godliness (1:3–4).

Scripture as the Predictions of the Holy Prophets and the Commandment of the Lord Jesus

When Peter refers to Scripture, it is natural to assume that he has in view what we know today as the Old Testament. But there are indications within 2 Peter that he understood God's word as having a twofold structure that anticipates what today we refer to as the Old and New Testaments.

The first passage to note is 2 Peter 3:2, where the apostle exhorts believers to "remember the predictions of the holy prophets and the commandment of the Lord and Savior through your apostles." The "predictions of the holy prophets" refers to the Old Testament in its totality, evidenced by Peter's use of specific texts from all three major divisions of the Hebrew canon (Torah, Prophets, and Writings).[8] As he had written previously, Peter was convinced that the Old Testament authors were serving present-day believers as they proclaimed the good news that God had revealed to them (1 Pet. 1:10–12, 22–25). Since the expression "predictions of the holy prophets" refers to written texts, there is good reason to conclude that the parallel expression "the commandment of the Lord and Savior through your apostles" also refers (at least in part) to written texts (cf. Jude 17).[9] The plural "apostles" further indicates an awareness of multiple divinely inspired and authoritative writings, including Peter's own letters.

The second text is found in the same chapter. Peter explains that "ignorant and unstable" people twist Paul's letters "to their own destruction, as they do the other Scriptures" (2 Pet. 3:16). Peter is not only aware of multiple Pauline letters but assumes that his readers are likewise aware of them and likely have access to them in some form. Even more significantly, Peter acknowledges that Paul's letters are regarded as inspired Scripture, of equal authority with the Old Testament writings.

8 In 2 Pet. 1:20 the apostle states that "no prophecy of Scripture comes from someone's own interpretation." That claim comes on the heels of describing Jesus's transfiguration, in which he alludes to or echoes texts from the Torah (Gen. 22), the Prophets (Isa. 42:1), and the Writings (Pss. 2, 8).

9 Michael J. Kruger, *The Question of Canon: Challenging the Status Quo in the New Testament Debate* (Downers Grove, IL: InterVarsity Press, 2013), 150.

Perhaps most noteworthy is that Peter can make such statements almost in passing. He makes no attempt to explain or defend the twofold nature of Scripture consisting of the Old Testament writings alongside the writings of the apostles. At the least this demonstrates a realization very early within the history of the church that God was speaking authoritatively through his apostolic witnesses as they wrote. The close association between God making a covenant with his people and then inspiring authoritative written documents in connection with that covenant is well-established in the Old Testament.[10] Recognizing that Jesus had inaugurated the new covenant with them, it makes sense that he would inspire authoritative written documents that explain that covenant and lay out the stipulations for how his covenant people should live.[11] Peter even frames this current letter as a "reminder" (1:13; 3:1) to enable the readers "at any time to recall these things" (1:15).

Thus there is every reason to see in what Peter says an early recognition of the twofold nature of Scripture, consisting of the Old Testament and the apostolic writings.

Excursus: What Books Counted as Scripture?

One of the more challenging theological issues to wrestle with in 2 Peter and Jude is their use of traditions and materials that are not found in the Old Testament. This challenge is most obvious in Jude, who not only draws on interpretive traditions found in noncanonical Jewish literature, but actually quotes from one such text. As part of his description of the false teachers, Jude writes:

10 On this point see especially Meredith G. Kline, *The Structure of Biblical Authority*, 2nd ed. (Eugene, OR: Wipf & Stock, 1989), 43–75.

11 For elaboration on this point, see Kruger, *Question of Canon*, 43–78.

> It was also about these that Enoch, the seventh from Adam, prophesied, saying, "Behold, the Lord comes with ten thousands of his holy ones, to execute judgment on all and to convict all the ungodly of all their deeds of ungodliness that they have committed in such an ungodly way, and of all the harsh things that ungodly sinners have spoken against him." (Jude 14–15)

According to Genesis 5:21–24, Enoch was the son of Methusaleh, the longest-living man mentioned in the Bible. What made Enoch unique was the fact that he did not die. In contrast to all the others mentioned in Genesis 5:1–31, "Enoch walked with God, and he was not, for God took him" (Gen. 5:24). Because Enoch was taken directly into heaven without dying, several traditions eventually arose surrounding him. Most of these traditions centered on Enoch receiving visions from angels (often called "watchers") that foretold events yet to come in God's plan for human history and in particular his people. Jude appears to quote from a document that came to be known as *1 Enoch*.[a] In the section Jude cites, the author describes the vision he received concerning God coming down from heaven to judge the entire earth (*1 En.* 1:1–9). When he descends, the earth will be destroyed and judgment will be announced. The righteous/elect will receive peace, kindness, blessing, and prosperity (*1 En.* 1:2–8). By contrast, the wicked (whether angelic or human) will be destroyed for their rebellion against God (*1 En.* 1:9). It is this last verse that Jude appears to quote in verses 14–15.

Less obvious are two places where Jude clearly draws on interpretive traditions drawn from Jewish literature not found in the Old Testament canon. The first is Jude 6 (cf. 2 Pet. 2:4), where he refers to angels "who did not stay within their own position of authority, but left their proper dwelling"; God "has kept [them] in eternal chains under gloomy darkness until the judgment of the great day." Jude is summarizing Genesis 6:1–4, where the "sons of God" take "the daughters of men" and in doing so incur God's judgment. But his summary of this event appears dependent upon Jewish interpretive traditions such as those found in *1 Enoch* 6–21.

The second is Jude 9, where he refers to events surrounding Moses's death. While Deuteronomy 34:1–12 records the death of Moses, Jewish literature went beyond what Scripture recounts in describing a dispute between the angel Michael and the devil over Moses's body. According to these traditions, the devil claimed he should have possession of Moses's body because Moses was a murderer (cf. Ex. 2:11). In response, Michael announces the Lord's rebuke on him, borrowing language from Zechariah 3:2. The Jewish traditions behind this story appear to come from a document known as *Testament of Moses*, which likely dates from around the time of Jesus's birth.[b]

At first glance, quoting from a source not found in our Bibles might seem troubling since it could give the impression that Jude considered *1 Enoch* canonical when we as believers today do not. But the fact that Peter and Jude include material in their writings that originates from noncanonical Jewish sources does not automatically mean they regarded those materials as inspired Scripture. Writing to Titus, the apostle Paul quotes the Greek poet Epimenides of Crete when he says, "Cretans are always liars, evil beasts, lazy gluttons" (Titus 1:12). In his message to the Athenians, Paul quotes the Greek poet Aratus when he says, "'In him we live and move and have our being'; as even some of your own poets have said, 'For we are indeed his offspring'" (Acts 17:28). Paul quotes these pagan authors because in that particular utterance he concluded that they said something true, not that their writings were inspired Scripture.

Second, there is compelling evidence that by the time of Jesus, the contours of the Old Testament canon were reasonably fixed.[c] There is no evidence from Jewish sources that suggests either *1 Enoch* or *Testament of Moses* were considered authoritative Scripture. When Jesus refers to "the blood of righteous Abel to the blood of Zechariah the son of Barachiah" (Matt. 23:35), he lists the first and last murders recorded in the Old Testament according to the Hebrew order of the books; in doing so he is making a reference to the totality of the Old Testament. The Jewish historian Josephus, writing in the late first century AD, lists the canonical books in a way that corresponds to our present-day Old Testament.

Third, even when Jude introduces his quotation from *1 Enoch* with the expression "Enoch, the seventh from Adam, prophesied" (Jude 14), this does not automatically mean that Jude regarded the book *1 Enoch* as authoritative Scripture. While this verb can be used to introduce a scriptural citation (e.g., Matt. 15:7; 1 Pet. 1:10), it also introduces the statement of Caiaphas the unbelieving high priest prophesying that Jesus would die for the nation (John 11:51).[d] As Richard Bauckham helpfully notes, at Qumran the scribes regularly interacted with and drew from the *Enoch* literature and other apocryphal works without regarding them as authoritative Scripture.[e]

a What we refer to today as *1 Enoch* is likely a collection of five distinct works that range in date from the fourth century BC to the first century AD. The particular section that Jude quotes from is known as "The Book of the Watchers" (*1 En.* 1–36), which can be dated sometime before the second century BC (several fragments were discovered among the Dead Sea Scrolls). The Book of the Watchers focuses on the fall of rebellious angels, their role in stirring up evil among mankind, and God's intention to judge both rebellious angels and sinful humanity. See further Daniel M. Gurtner, *Introducing the Pseudepigrapha of Second Temple Judaism: Message, Context, and Significance* (Grand Rapids, MI: Baker Academic, 2020), 21–91.

b For a helpful introduction to *Testament of Moses*, see Gurtner, *Introducing the Pseudepigrapha*, 167–76. For an attempt to reconstruct the background and source of the text behind Jude 9, see Richard Bauckham, *Jude, 2 Peter*, WBC 50 (Dallas: Word, 1990), 65–76.

c On this important topic, see Roger T. Beckwith, *The Old Testament Canon of the New Testament Church and Its Background in Early Judaism* (Grand Rapids, MI: Eerdmans, 1986); E. Earle Ellis, *The Old Testament in Early Christianity: Canon and Interpretation in the Light of Modern Research* (Grand Rapids, MI: Baker, 1992); and especially Stephen Dempster, "The Old Testament Canon, Josephus, and Cognitive Framework," in *The Enduring Authority of the Christian Scriptures*, ed. D. A. Carson (Grand Rapids, MI: Eerdmans, 2016), 321–61.

d Thomas R. Schreiner, *1–2 Peter and Jude*, Christian Standard Commentary (Nashville, TN: B&H, 2020), 569.

e Richard Bauckham, *Jude and the Relatives of Jesus in the Early Church* (London: T&T Clark, 2004), 25–33.

Conclusion

The same God who spoke all things into existence has spoken through his word. Peter and Jude show an unshakable confidence in Scripture. Not only do they believe it is truthful and reliable; they believe it is powerful and sufficient. It explains what God has done for his people and instructs us how to live. Scripture is both truthful and reliable, providing us with the spiritual food we need to live as God's people in a fallen world that desperately needs to hear the good news of what God has done in and through Jesus Christ.

2

The God Who Judges and Saves

A. W. TOZER FAMOUSLY WROTE THAT "what comes into our minds when we think about God is the most important thing about us."[1] Unfortunately, what comes to mind for many people is what sociologists Christian Smith and Melinda Lundquist Denton have summarized as "moralistic therapeutic deism."[2] They summarize the basic tenets as follows:[3]

1. A God exists who created and orders the world and watches over human life on earth.
2. God wants people to be good, nice, and fair to each other, as taught in the Bible and by most world religions.
3. The central goal of life is to be happy and to feel good about oneself.
4. God does not need to be particularly involved in one's life except when God is needed to resolve a problem.
5. Good people go to heaven when they die.

1 A. W. Tozer, *The Knowledge of the Holy*, 1st HarperCollins gift ed. (New York: HarperSanFrancisco, 1992), 1.

2 Christian Smith and Melinda Lundquist Denton, *Soul Searching: The Religious and Spiritual Lives of American Teenagers* (Oxford, UK: Oxford University Press, 2005). Although this study focused on teenagers, others have rightly pointed out the presence of this perspective throughout the American church. See, e.g., Kenda Creasy Dean, *Almost Christian: What the Faith of Our Teenagers Is Telling the American Church* (Oxford, UK: Oxford University Press, 2010).

3 Smith and Denton, *Soul Searching*, 162–63.

Given this broad framework that characterizes many within our culture and even within the church, it is all the more important that we have a truly biblical understanding of who God is.

One outworking of moralistic therapeutic deism is that judging others is one of the greatest sins one can commit. Yet the moment we are wronged, we feel an instinctive desire for that wrong to be made right. The greater the wrong, the more intense that desire for someone to make things right. Our God-given sense of the need for justice remains in every single individual, no matter how aggressive the attempt to suppress it.

To help us see more clearly who God is in 2 Peter and Jude, we will first look at the triune identity of the one true God. Then we will explore how God reveals himself as the one who saves his people and judges his enemies.

The Triune God on Display

Throughout both 2 Peter and Jude we see all three persons of the Trinity actively working together to accomplish God's purposes. At times Peter and Jude highlight the actions of one particular member of the Trinity, while at other times they simply refer in a broad way to God without distinguishing which particular person is in view. But a good starting point will be to summarize what Peter and Jude say about each person of the Trinity before moving toward synthesis.

God the Father. Although the Father is only explicitly mentioned once in each book (2 Pet. 1:17; Jude 1), there are additional passages that one can infer refer more specifically to him. A good place to begin is that the Father possesses unrivaled glory. Indeed, Peter explicitly refers to God the Father as "the Majestic Glory" in his description of the transfiguration (2 Pet. 1:17). Jude concludes his letter with a benediction that ascribes to God the Father "glory, majesty, dominion, and authority, before all time and now and forever. Amen" (Jude 25). The Father not only delights in the Son but publicly affirms his identity at the transfiguration (2 Pet. 1:17–18).

When it comes to redemption, God the Father is involved from start to finish. He is the one who effectually calls those whom he elected to be his people and sets his love upon them (1:10; cf. 1 Pet. 1:15; 2:9; 5:10; Jude 1). The Father not only makes promises that he is faithful to fulfill (2 Pet. 1:19; 3:9–13), but he also gave his words to men who wrote them down as authoritative Scripture (1:21). What might seem on the surface to be a delay in the Father fulfilling his promises is in fact an expression of his patient love, providing time for people to repent before the day of judgment (3:8–13). As a result, Jude 25 refers to him as our Savior.

God the Son. Without question God the Son is at the center of what 2 Peter and Jude have to say about God. A good place to start our exploration is to note that the Son shares the Father's glory. At the transfiguration the Son "received honor and glory from God the Father" (2 Pet. 1:17). This is glory that the Son shares with the Father "both now and to the day of eternity" (3:18). Isaiah 42:8, however, makes it clear that Yahweh does not share his glory with anyone else: "I am the LORD; that is my name; my glory I give to no other, nor my praise to carved idols." So the fact that the Son shares in the glory of the Father indicates that the Son is fully God just as the Father is.

The most prominent title for God the Son in 2 Peter and Jude is "Lord" (Gk. *kyrios*). While it is true that this Greek word is used in a wide variety of ways, it is important to note that it was consistently used in the LXX (the Greek translation of the Hebrew Old Testament) to translate God's special covenant name (Heb. *yhwh*).[4] Applying this title to Jesus is an additional indicator of the Son's full deity, stressing his complete authority over not just his people, but creation itself (2 Pet. 1:2, 8, 14, 16; 3:2; Jude 17, 25). He exercises this authority over an eternal kingdom where he alone determines who enters and who does not (2 Pet. 1:11). The Son's divine authority is further brought out by referring to him as "Master" (Gk. *despotēs*), another term depicting Jesus's comprehensive authority. Although less common than "Lord" in the LXX, this Greek word is used as a title for God

4 In most English translations this name is rendered as LORD in small caps, distinguishing it from the title Lord (a separate Hebrew word). This divine name is also commonly transliterated as Yahweh or Jehovah.

as well (see, e.g., Gen. 15:2, 8; Josh. 5:14; Isa. 3:1; Jer. 1:6; 4:10). Those who claim to know Jesus but deny him through their false beliefs and immoral lifestyles reject his authority as Master (2 Pet. 2:1; Jude 4).

As Lord and Master, Jesus Christ has not only the authority to rule over creation but the power to do so. Peter characterizes the entirety of Jesus's life and ministry as "the power and coming of our Lord Jesus Christ" (2 Pet. 1:16). He uses this power in several distinct ways. First, he uses it to save his people. Indeed, Jude takes great pains to remind his readers "that Jesus, who saved a people out of the land of Egypt, afterward destroyed those who did not believe" (Jude 5).[5] Jude in essence pulls back the curtain to show us that God the Son not only redeemed believers from their captivity to sin through a new exodus but was the one who led Israel out of Egypt in the original exodus. It is the Son's divine power that "has granted to us all things that pertain to life and godliness, through the knowledge of him who called us to his own glory and excellence" (2 Pet. 1:3). His power enables the Son to keep believers from stumbling and present them blameless before the Father on the last day (Jude 1, 23). In light of this holistic work to transform rebellious sinners into a holy people, preserve them as they live in this fallen world, and present them blameless before the Father on the last day, it is no wonder that the Son is called our Lord and Savior (2 Pet. 1:1, 11; 2:20; 3:2, 18).

God the Holy Spirit. Although the Spirit is not absent from 2 Peter and Jude, he receives the least explicit attention of the persons within the Trinity. The Spirit was intimately involved in the production of Scripture. He is the one who "carried along" the men who wrote down God's word at his direction (2 Pet. 1:21). Similar language is found in both Josephus (*Ant.* 4.119) and Philo (*Spec.* 1.65) to describe God's Spirit working in the human authors to produce Scripture. This contention is consistent with what Peter wrote in his first letter, where he explains that the prophets were "inquiring what person or time the Spirit of Christ in them was indicating when he predicted the suffer-

5 On the significant textual variant here, see discussion below.

ings of Christ and the subsequent glories" (1 Pet. 1:11). It is this same Spirit that speaks through the preaching of the gospel today (cf. 1 Pet. 1:12–13, 22–25). The Holy Spirit also empowers the prayers of God's people as a means of keeping them in God's love as they await the return of Christ (Jude 20–21).

The Triune God in Action. Perhaps the clearest passage that expresses a nascent Trinitarianism is Jude 20–21. After warning of worldly people who cause division, Jude directly addresses his audience:

> But you, beloved, building yourselves up in your most holy faith and praying in the Holy Spirit, keep yourselves in the love of God, waiting for the mercy of our Lord Jesus Christ that leads to eternal life.

The central exhortation is "keep yourselves in the love of God." Jude gives three ways that believers do this: (1) building yourselves up in your faith; (2) praying in the Holy Spirit; and (3) waiting for the mercy of our Lord Jesus Christ. If we recognize that in this context "God" refers to the Father, then we can easily recognize the Trinitarian shape of Jude's exhortation. God the Father is the one who set his love upon us. His Son the Lord Jesus Christ is the one who will show us mercy that leads to eternal life when he returns. The Holy Spirit empowers our prayers. Each person of the Trinity may have his own distinct role within the plan of redemption, but they work in concert as one God to accomplish all that God has purposed for us.

Other passages mention two persons of the Trinity. One of the clearest examples is Peter's description of the transfiguration, where the Father proclaims Jesus as his beloved Son, the promised Davidic king, and the Isaianic servant (2 Pet. 1:16–18). The production of Scripture is attributed to God (likely a reference to the Father) working in conjunction with the Holy Spirit (2 Pet. 1:21). Because believers are beloved by God (again, likely a reference to the Father), they are "kept for [/by] Jesus Christ" (Jude 1). Those who distort the grace of God into sensuality deny Jesus Christ as their Lord and Master (4).

While we do not find a fully developed Trinitarianism (as expressed in later technical formulations of the third and fourth centuries), the building blocks of those later formulations are certainly evident in 2 Peter and Jude. There is one God who exists in three persons who work together to accomplish God's purposes for the world.

The Pattern of God's Salvation and Judgment

A prominent theme that runs through the entirety of both 2 Peter and Jude is God saving his people and judging his enemies. Indeed, a close look at the overlapping material between these two letters reveals that these twin themes are central to the message of each epistle. Therefore understanding these two themes and their relationship to each other is foundational for a firm grasp of 2 Peter and Jude. But the significant amount of overlap between these two letters could obscure some of the subtle but significant differences between 2 Peter and Jude. To help mitigate such a danger, we will look at each account separately before attempting a synthesis.[6]

Jude. The brother of Jesus begins by expressing his desire to write about their common salvation; circumstances, however, compel him to call for his readers to contend for the "faith that was once for all delivered to the saints" (3) in light of the threat from false teachers "who pervert the grace of our God into sensuality" (4). With this foundation in place, Jude launches into his description and condemnation of the false teachers (5–16), which itself can be divided into three distinct sections.

6 The overlap in material raises the question of the literary relationship between 2 Peter and Jude. Three options are possible: (1) Peter uses Jude; (2) Jude uses Peter; or (3) Peter and Jude use a common source. Despite the amount of scholarship devoted to the issue, a consensus remains elusive; for a helpful summary of the issues, see Thomas R. Schreiner, *1–2 Peter and Jude*, Christian Standard Commentary (Nashville, TN: B&H, 2020), 499–503. On the whole, it seems more likely to me that Peter used Jude. For a robust discussion that reaches a similar conclusion, see Tommy Wasserman, *The Epistle of Jude: Its Text and Transmission*, ConBNT 43 (Stockholm, SE: Almqvist & Wiksell, 2006), 73–98. Because any conclusion on the relationship between 2 Peter and Jude must be provisional and tentative, I have tried to avoid conclusions that are dependent on a particular view.

First, the false teachers are destined for condemnation (5–10). Jude uses three typological examples from the Old Testament and one from extrabiblical Jewish tradition. His starting point is the exodus, Israel's paradigmatic redemptive act: "Now I want to remind you, although you once fully knew it, that Jesus, who saved a people out of the land of Egypt, afterward destroyed those who did not believe" (5).[7] Jude brings together the twin themes of salvation and judgment. As Israel's experience in the wilderness amply demonstrated, not everyone who was rescued from Egypt through the exodus made it to the promised land. Indeed, an entire generation (with only a few exceptions) experienced the judgment of God in the form of death in the wilderness because they failed to believe him and his promises (Num. 13–14). Moving backward in redemptive history, Jude's next example is the rebellious angels described in Genesis 6:1–4, who "did not stay within their own position of authority" and have since been chained in darkness until the judgment on the last day (Jude 6). The third typological example is similar. Sodom and Gomorrah were consumed by a punishment of eternal fire for their sexual immorality (7), the same fate that awaits the false teachers for their immorality (8). Jude concludes this section with an example from Jewish tradition. While arguing over the dead body of Moses, the archangel Michael refused to "pronounce a blasphemous judgment" (9), unlike the false teachers, who "blaspheme all that they do not understand" (10).

Second, the false teachers live ungodly lives (11–13). In this section Jude uses a combination of vivid metaphors and Old Testament

7 The Greek text of verse 5 contains one of the most well-known textual variants in Jude. Instead of saying that "Jesus" saved the Israelites out of Egypt, other manuscripts say it was "God" and still others say it was "the Lord." For helpful summaries of the textual evidence for each variant, see Wasserman, *Epistle of Jude*, 148–49; Gene L. Green, *Jude and 2 Peter*, BECNT (Grand Rapids, MI: Baker Academic, 2008), 64–65; and Herbert W. Bateman IV, *Jude*, EEC (Bellingham, WA: Lexham Press, 2017), 160–62. Even if Bateman is correct that "Lord" is the original reading (against the reading of the Greek New Testament [NA[28]]), it should be noted that it is still likely a reference to Jesus in light of Jude's consistent pattern of applying the title "Lord" to Jesus (4, 21, 25). Indeed, the fact that the last clause of verse 4 explicitly refers to "our only Master and Lord, Jesus Christ" leads the reader to conclude that the "Lord" in view is Jesus Christ rather than a general reference to God.

types to describe the false teachers' ungodly lifestyle. As in the previous section, Jude uses three typological examples from the Old Testament. They have "walked in the way of Cain" (11), a reference to Adam and Eve's oldest son, who killed his brother Abel in a fit of jealous rage (Gen. 4:1–16). As such he was also "the progenitor of covenant unfaithfulness."[8] Jude may rely in part here on Jewish tradition, which attributed to Cain greed, violence, lust, and, perhaps most pertinent for Jude, leading people into wickedness.[9] The false teachers have also "abandoned themselves for the sake of gain to Balaam's error" (Jude 11). While Israel wandered in the wilderness, Balak king of Moab paid the prophet Balaam to prophesy a curse over Israel (Num. 22–24). The false teachers share his greed as their motivation. The final Old Testament type that helps explain the behavior of the false teachers afflicting Jude's audience is Korah's rebellion (Jude 11). Shortly after refusing to enter the promised land, Korah gathered 250 chiefs of the congregation to rebel against the authority of Moses and Aaron, arguing that they had wrongly exalted themselves above the people (Num. 16:1–30). Yahweh vindicated Moses and Aaron by causing the ground to swallow Korah and all his followers (Num. 16:31–35). Since these false teachers follow in the pattern of Korah by speaking in a way that undermines the authority of church leaders, they too will perish in God's judgment.[10]

In addition to these typological examples, Jude uses six metaphors to describe the false teachers, with all but one coming from the realm

8 Brandon D. Crowe, *The Message of the General Epistles in the History of Redemption: Wisdom from James, Peter, John, and Jude* (Phillipsburg, NJ: P&R, 2015), 108. Crowe goes on to note, "Perhaps Jude would even have us make the connection between the reprobate line of Cain in contrast to the righteous line of Seth that leads to the Messiah" (110).

9 Richard Bauckham, *Jude, 2 Peter*, WBC 50 (Dallas: Word, 1990), 79–80. He notes the following texts: *Jub.* 4:31; *T. Benj.* 7:1–5; *Apoc. Ab.* 24:3–5; *Apoc. Mos.* 2:1–4; 3:1–3; 40:4–5; *1 En.* 22:7.

10 According to Bauckham (*Jude, 2 Peter*, 83), Korah "became the classic example of the antinomian heretic" in Jewish tradition. In using the Greek word *antilogia* to depict the rebellion, Jude likely highlights the key role that the speech of the false teachers plays in their efforts to undermine church leaders.

of nature.[11] As hidden reefs during the celebration of the Lord's Supper (Jude 12), the treachery of the false teachers lies just below the surface, destroying the unsuspecting. Calling them "shepherds feeding themselves" (12) indicates that rather than using positions of influence and leadership to care for others, the false teachers instead exploit God's people for their own selfish benefit (cf. Ezek. 34:1–8). "Waterless clouds, swept along by winds" (Jude 12) portrays the empty promises of what the false teachers offer. They lack the life-giving sustenance of the living water of the gospel, and thus they are blown around aimlessly by the winds of personal whims and doctrinal confusion. Instead of bearing good fruit as evidence of a changed heart (Luke 6:43–45), the opponents are "fruitless trees in late autumn, twice dead, uprooted" (Jude 12). Late autumn is the time when trees bear fruit, so its absence demonstrates the utter spiritual deadness of the opponents. The volatility and uncontrolled immoral behavior of the false teachers is portrayed as "wild waves of the sea, casting up the foam of their own shame" (13). Just as waves dredge filth from the bottom of the sea and toss it to the surface, so the ungodliness of the false teachers overflows into public view. Lastly, the false teachers are "wandering stars, for whom the gloom of utter darkness has been reserved forever" (13). Unlike the saints, who will shine like stars in the resurrection (Dan. 12:3), the false teachers have departed from their proper sphere and thus merit judgment.

Third, the false teachers will be judged on the last day (Jude 14–16). Jude supports this claim by referring to Enoch, "the seventh from Adam," who prophesied this judgment. According to Genesis 5:24, "Enoch walked with God, and he was not, for God took him." Thus unlike the other figures listed in the genealogy of Genesis 5:1–32, Enoch did not die. Instead, he was taken directly into heaven by God. As noted in the previous chapter (see excursus), a significant tradition arose within Jewish literature that portrayed Enoch as the recipient of

11 This paragraph is adapted from Matthew S. Harmon, "Jude," in *Hebrews–Revelation*, ed. Iain M. Duguid, James M. Hamilton, and Jay Sklar, vol. 12, ESV Expository Commentary (Wheaton, IL: Crossway, 2018), 516.

heavenly visions and revelations.[12] Drawing from what has come to be known as *1 Enoch*, Jude asserts that Enoch prophesied about the judgment that awaits these false teachers:

> Behold, the Lord comes with ten thousands of his holy ones, to execute judgment on all and to convict all the ungodly of all their deeds of ungodliness that they have committed in such an ungodly way, and of all the harsh things that ungodly sinners have spoken against him. (Jude 14–15)[13]

While there is little question the wording comes from *1 Enoch*, the ideas and concepts themselves are firmly rooted within the Old Testament itself. The presence of "ten thousands of his holy ones" likely echoes the description of God's appearance at Sinai with the angelic host (Deut. 33:2; cf. Dan. 7:10). Descriptions of Yahweh coming to judge the earth and all its inhabitants are common in the Old Testament, especially in the psalms (e.g., Pss. 58:11; 96:13; 98:9) and the prophets (e.g., Isa. 24:1–23; Joel 2:1–11; Zeph. 1:2–18). Perhaps even more interesting is that Jude takes language that in *1 Enoch* refers to God coming to judge and instead identifies "the Lord" (Gk. *kyrios*) as the one who executes this judgment. While this could simply be a generic reference to God, given Jude's consistent application of this title to Jesus it seems more likely that Jude is claiming that the Lord Jesus Christ will be the one to execute God's judgment.[14] The very Jesus these false teachers deny as "Master and

12 For a helpful summary of Enoch in Jewish literature, see Bateman, *Jude*, 302–12.

13 The wording of this citation seems to most closely match the Greek version of *1 Enoch*; for further discussion, see Bateman, *Jude*, 310–19.

14 Of the six occurrences of "Lord" (Gk. *kyrios*) in Jude, four are explicit references to Jesus Christ (4, 17, 21, 25). Only verse 9, where Michael pronounces, "The Lord rebuke you," seems likely to be a generic reference to God, though even here one wonders if Jude sees in this a reference to Christ. On verse 14 as a reference to Jesus Christ, see Bateman, *Jude*, 313–14. Bateman helpfully notes that other NT authors "make similar referent shifts from God to Jesus concerning future judgments" (314). In 2 Peter, all fourteen uses of "Lord" may refer to Jesus; see Peter H. Davids, *A Theology of James, Peter, and Jude*, BTNT 6 (Grand Rapids, MI: Zondervan, 2014), 234.

Lord" (Jude 4) will be the one who executes judgment on them for their lies and immorality.

From this condemnation of the false teachers Jude moves on to exhort believers to persevere in the true faith (17–23). They must remember "the predictions of the apostles of our Lord Jesus Christ" (17) regarding the arrival of ungodly scoffers who would cause division (18–19). By contrast, Jude exhorts believers to "keep yourselves in the love of God" (21). They do so by building themselves up in their faith (20), praying in the Holy Spirit (20), and waiting for the mercy of the Lord Jesus on the last day (21). As they have opportunity they should show mercy to those who are wavering in the faith and seek to restore those on the path to destruction through their unrepentant sin (22–23).

Jude concludes with a stirring doxology that focuses on God's power and glory (24–25). Despite the very real danger posed by the false teachers, God is able to preserve believers until the last, when they will appear before God blameless and joyful (24). Because of this, God is worthy of all "glory, majesty, dominion, and authority, before all time and now and forever. Amen" (25).

Second Peter. Peter begins the letter with a call to pursue growth in godliness as a means to making one's calling and election sure (1:1–11), followed by a statement of his intent to perpetually remind his readers of the truth of the gospel through this letter, even after his death (1:12–15). The letter body begins with a paragraph that grounds the truth of the gospel in the apostle's eyewitness testimony and the fulfillment of Old Testament promises (1:16–21).

It is against this backdrop that Peter addresses the presence and problem of false teachers (2:1–3:13). He begins by noting the certainty of false teachers arising (2:1–3a), a certainty that rests on the existence of false prophets among the people of Israel. These contemporary false teachers secretly introduce destructive heresies and deny Christ as their Master through their sensual lifestyle. Motivated by greed they use smooth words to exploit God's people and entice them to follow in their sensuality.

With the stage now set, Peter asserts the certainty of God's judgment on false teachers and his preservation of his people (2:3b–10a). After an initial statement of assurance that God's condemnation of such false teachers is certain (2:3b), Peter highlights a series of Old Testament examples that illustrate this central point.[15] The initial example is that of angels who sinned being cast into hell and bound with chains until the day of judgment. This appears to be a summary of Genesis 6:1–4, where the sons of God (i.e., angels) took the daughters of men as wives and produced offspring, though Peter's summary appears influenced by noncanonical Jewish literature and interpretive traditions.[16] The second example is that of God destroying the ancient world with a flood but preserving Noah and his family through it (2 Pet. 2:5). This summary of Genesis 6:5–9:17 highlights Noah as a "herald of righteousness" to portray him as a precursor to present-day preachers of the gospel who announce God's righteousness revealed in and through Jesus Christ (cf. 2 Pet. 1:1). For his third example (2:6–8), Peter draws from the story of Sodom and Gomorrah (Gen. 18–19). God condemning these two cities to extinction was intended as an example that anticipated the even greater eternal destruction that awaits the ungodly on the last day. By contrast, God rescued "righteous Lot," whose soul was constantly tormented over the wickedness around him. Based on these Old Testament examples, Peter confidently asserts that "the Lord knows how to rescue the godly from trials, and to keep the unrighteous under punishment until the day of judgment" (2 Pet. 2:9). That is the central point Peter wants his readers to grasp. God has a proven track record of judging his enemies and saving his people. As a result, they can be confident that no matter how successful the false teachers appear to be, God will preserve his people through these trials and eternally condemn the false teachers. Such condemnation

15 Verses 4–10a are one long sentence in Greek, structured as a complex first-class conditional statement, presenting the "if" statements as true for the sake of the argument. Based on the truth of those "if" statements (2:4–8), Peter draws a logical conclusion (2:9–10a).

16 For a helpful discussion of this passage see Schreiner, *1–2 Peter and Jude*, 401–4, 539–44. As he notes, the traditions connected with this story were well known in the ancient world, even outside of Jewish circles.

will be especially fitting for "those who indulge in the lust of defiling passion and despise authority" (2:10a).

The mention of their wickedness and sensuality leads to a scathing description of the false teachers (2:10b–22), filled with colorful language and some additional Old Testament examples. According to 2:10b–11, in their arrogance they slander evil spiritual beings and dismiss "the possibility that their sins might put them at the mercy of such evil spiritual beings."[17] Because they follow their sinful desires and are controlled by their passions, the false teachers are like irrational animals destined for destruction who even now are experiencing the consequences of their immorality and greed (2:12–14). To further illustrate the waywardness of the false teachers, Peter compares them to Balaam (2:15–16), the false prophet whom the king of Moab hired to curse Israel in the wilderness (Num. 22–24). While on the way to pronounce a curse on Israel, God rebuked Balaam through the words of the donkey he was riding on (Num. 22:22–41). Peter sees in the false teachers the same greed and rebellion that motivated Balaam. Despite the confident boasts of the false teachers that they promote the path to freedom, they instead are leading people back down the path of slavery to the very defilements that Christ delivers from through the gospel (2 Pet. 2:17–20). Those who follow their path will find themselves worse off than if they had never heard the gospel (2:21); as such they are like dogs returning to their vomit and pigs wallowing in the mud after being washed (2:22).

It is not merely the ungodliness of the false teachers that must be exposed. Peter next moves to expose and correct their aberrant doctrine (3:1–13). The key to identifying their false teaching is remembering the twofold witness of "the holy prophets" and the words of Jesus as taught through the apostles (3:1–2). Together they had warned that scoffers would arise who cynically dismiss the second coming of Christ (3:3–4). Peter highlights that such scoffers deliberately overlook the fact that

17 Peter's precise meaning here is debated. For a helpful discussion that reaches a similar conclusion, see Douglas J. Moo, *2 Peter, Jude: From Biblical Text to Contemporary Life*, NIVAC (Grand Rapids, MI: Zondervan, 1996), 123.

the world that God created out of water through his word was deluged by that same water and word (3:5–6). It is that same word of God that is preserving the present creation for a fiery judgment on the last day (3:7). To combat this false teaching Peter reminds believers that God transcends time (3:8), and his apparent slowness to keep his promises provides more people with time to repent (3:9). One day, however, God's patience will be exhausted, Jesus will return like a thief in the night, and the present creation will undergo a fiery judgment in which everything will be exposed (3:10). In light of these realities, God's people should live lives of holiness as they eagerly anticipate a new creation in which righteousness dwells (3:11–13).

Peter concludes the letter with an exhortation to live godly lives as they patiently await Christ's return (3:14–18). They must diligently pursue peaceful lives that are "without spot or blemish" (3:14). God's patience is leading more people to be saved, a point that the apostle Paul also makes, though those who are ignorant and unstable twist his words just as they do the rest of Scripture (3:15–16). But rather than being carried away by the errors of such rebellious people, believers must grow in the grace and knowledge of Jesus Christ (3:17). He alone deserves eternal glory (3:18).

Synthesis. After working through the relevant sections of 2 Peter and Jude the overlap is evident (see table 1).

Table 1

Topic	2 Peter	Jude
False teachers arise who deny our Master and Lord Jesus Christ and were marked for destruction long ago	2:1–3	4
Jesus saved a people out of Egypt and then destroyed those who did not believe		5
Angels who went beyond their appointed boundaries were kept in darkness for judgment on the last day (Gen. 6:1–4)	2:4	6
God preserved Noah through the flood that destroyed the world	2:5	
Sodom and Gomorrah were destroyed because of their immorality as an example of eternal destruction	2:6	7

Table 1 (*continued*)

Topic	2 Peter	Jude
God rescued righteous Lot, who was distressed by the ungodliness and sensuality of the wicked around him	2:7–8	
The Lord knows how to rescue the godly from trials and keep the unrighteous under punishment for the day of judgment	2:9	
Present-day false teachers indulge/defile the flesh and revile angelic majesties	2:10	8
Though greater in power, Michael/angels do not dare pronounce judgment against rebellious angels	2:11	9
Present-day false teachers revile what they do not understand and are like unreasoning animals headed for destruction	2:12	10
Present-day false teachers are described in a poetic manner	2:13–14	
Present-day false teachers have gone the way of Cain		11a
Present-day false teachers have followed the way of Balaam	2:15–16	11b
Present-day false teachers have followed the path of rebellion marked out by Korah		11c
Present-day false teachers are described in a poetic manner	2:17	12–13
Enoch prophesied about these false teachers		14–15
Present-day false teachers are described in poetic manner with a focus on their speech (arrogant, deceptive)	2:18	16
Present-day false teachers promise freedom but are slaves to corruption	2:19	
Explanation → those who claim to know Christ and then are overcome by defilements of the flesh are worse off than before they encountered Christ	2:20–22	
Exhortation → remember the words of the prophets and the apostles that mockers following after their own lusts would come in the last days	3:1–3	17–19
These mockers deny the return of Christ and the promise of a new creation	3:4–10	
Exhortation → pursue a life of holiness / keep yourself in the love of God	3:11–13	20–23
Reminder → diligently pursue godliness and beware of those who twist the Scriptures	3:14–17	
Benediction → to God alone be glory forever	3:18	24–25

Both are deeply concerned about the presence of people who at some level claim to be followers of Christ but in fact deny him through false teaching and ungodly living. Indeed, for both Peter and Jude ungodliness is the preferred summary term for the errant ways of the opponents.[18] If godliness refers to orienting the totality of one's life to God such that one's thoughts, inclinations, attitudes, beliefs, and actions are united toward the worship of our Lord and Savior Jesus Christ, then those who fail to submit to his authority as Lord and Master are by definition ungodly. Although they claim to know Christ, their ungodliness reveals just how unlike Jesus they actually are. Those who genuinely follow the one who perfectly loved God with his whole heart, mind, and strength and his neighbor as himself will live lives that reflect that same Godward orientation of life.

Central to the shared message of 2 Peter and Jude is the assurance that God will bring judgment on those who not only rebel against his moral standards but also entice others to follow them in their ungodliness. This conviction rests on the clear pattern demonstrated in several examples from both the Old Testament and noncanonical Jewish literature that were well known to their respective audiences. But these are more than simple illustrations. Peter and Jude see in these examples an anticipation of God's decisive judgment on all who reject his authority and transgress the boundaries he has rightly established (2 Pet. 2:6; 3:5–7; Jude 8, 11, 14–15). Put another way, these are types that will have their fulfillment in the judgment that takes place on the climactic day of the Lord at the end of human history (2 Pet. 3:10; Jude 6, 14–15).

Peter and Jude are not all doom and gloom, however. Without in any way downplaying the terrifying reality of judgment, both authors also emphasize God's desire and power to save his people. This salva-

18 Peter uses different members of the Greek word family for *ungodly* three times: the adjective (*asebēs*) occurs twice (2:5; 3:7) and the verb (*asebeō*) once (2:6). These descriptions are intentionally contrasted with believers, who are referred to as godly (*eusebēs*; 2:9) and are called to pursue godliness (*eusebeia*; 1:3, 6–7; 3:11). Jude uses the word family a total of five times in his short letter: the adjective (*asebēs*) occurs twice (4, 15), the noun (*asebeia*) occurs twice (15, 18), and the verb (*asebeō*) once (15). In contrast to 2 Peter, Jude never uses the positive terms *godly* or *godliness*.

tion has past, present, and future dimensions. Salvation is something that in one sense has already happened. Through the righteousness of Jesus and our knowledge of him, God has rescued his people from the corruption of this world that comes from sinful desires (2 Pet. 1:1, 4, 9; 2:20). This salvation is our common experience as believers, the glue that binds us together as God's people (Jude 3). Yet believers are also in the process of being saved from the sinful desires that remain. God has given believers everything necessary for life and godliness through his promises, which make us "partakers of the divine nature" (2 Pet. 1:3–4). Based on these promises believers must pursue growth in qualities such as virtue, knowledge, self-control, steadfastness, godliness, brotherly affection, and love (1:5–8). Believers keep themselves in the love of God by building up their holy faith and praying in the Spirit (Jude 20–21), pursuing the goal of being found blameless on the last day (24). The future aspect of salvation is expressed in multiple ways. It is an "entrance into the eternal kingdom of our Lord and Savior Jesus Christ" (2 Pet. 1:11). Put another way, our future salvation culminates in a "new heavens and a new earth in which righteousness dwells" (3:13; cf. Isa. 32:16; 60:21; 65:17–25). On that last day God will present his people "blameless before the presence of his glory with great joy" (Jude 24). Even the seeming delay in Christ's return is rooted in God's desire "that all should reach repentance" (2 Pet. 3:9). From start to finish and every point in between, salvation is a work of God.

Within this significant overlap of material, however, Peter and Jude each have their distinctive elements. Peter consistently interlaces God saving his people and judging his enemies (2:3a–10a), moving seamlessly back and forth between the two. Jude, by contrast, begins with a statement combining God saving his people and bringing judgment on his enemies (Jude 5) but then quickly moves on to an extended section that discusses only judgment (6–16). Jude begins his series of Old Testament types with the exodus (5), likely seeing it as a key paradigm to understand what Jesus has done for the church. Peter does not use the exodus as part of his series of Old Testament types that point to God's even greater acts of salvation and judgment. However, Peter does use exodus language in connection with his impending death (2 Pet. 1:15), and his use of the transfiguration (1:16–21) may have faint exodus overtones as well if understood in light of Luke's account (Luke 9:28–36), which does use exodus language (Luke 9:31). Peter also includes two examples that Jude does not: the flood (2 Pet. 2:5) and God's rescue of Lot (2:7–8).

Peter and Jude also use different vocabulary to describe both salvation and judgment. Peter is especially fond of "righteousness" language.[19] It is the righteousness of God that has given us our standing before God (1:1) and the way by which believers walk (2:21). Noah was a "herald of righteousness" (2:5), and twice Lot (despite his obvious shortcomings!) is described as righteous (2:7–8). The new creation that believers await is described as a place where righteousness dwells (3:13). Those who rebel against God's authority are unrighteous (2:9) and suffer wrong for their unrighteousness (2:13) as they pursue gain from their unrighteousness (2:15). By contrast, Jude uses such language only once in describing the punishment on Sodom and Gomorrah (Jude 7).

Conclusion

The God of the Bible is not the god depicted in moralistic therapeutic deism. Far from being an uninvolved deity who simply wants people to get along and play nice with each other, the God of the Bible reveals himself as both a savior and a judge. He is one God, but he exists as three distinct persons—Father, Son, and Spirit. All three persons of the Trinity work in harmony to save his people from their sin and the righteous wrath they deserve. Those who refuse to repent of their sin and reject his authority over their lives face the certain prospect of terrifying eternal judgment. Just as the Old Testament revealed, God saves his people and judges his enemies as a manifestation of his own righteousness.

19 Specifically, he frequently uses words from the Greek word family *dik-* throughout his letter: *dikaiosynē* (1:1; 2:5, 21; 3:13); *dikaios* (1:13; 2:7–8); *adikos* (2:9), *adikeō* (2:13), *adikia* (2:13, 15).

3

False Teaching

ONE OF THE CONSTANT CHALLENGES that God's people have had to face is false teaching. In one sense it can seem like there are new variations of false teaching that arise on a regular basis, and there is an element of truth to that. Satan often finds new and innovative ways to challenge the truth of God's word in an effort to deceive people, especially those who follow Christ. Yet in another sense, what often seem to be new forms of false teaching are in fact repackaged versions of heretical ideas that the church has already dealt with at some point in her long history. Although not specifically talking about false teaching, the words of Ecclesiastes 1:9 ring particularly true with regard to false teaching: "What has been is what will be, and what has been done is what will be done, and there is nothing new under the sun."

Despite the claims of some scholars that there was no clearly fixed "orthodoxy" in the first century,[1] the authors of the New Testament epistles regularly address and correct aberrant beliefs and practices that are inconsistent with the truth of the gospel proclaimed by Jesus and preached by the apostles. Peter and Jude are no different. In an effort

1 The most prominent mainstream advocate of this view is Bart Ehrman; see especially Bart D. Ehrman, *Lost Christianities: The Battles for Scripture and the Faiths We Never Knew* (New York: Oxford University Press, 2003). For a helpful summary and substantive critique of Ehrman's view, see Andreas J. Köstenberger and Michael J. Kruger, *The Heresy of Orthodoxy: How Contemporary Culture's Fascination with Diversity Has Reshaped Our Understanding of Early Christianity* (Wheaton, IL: Crossway, 2010).

to summarize what 2 Peter and Jude say about false teaching, we will look at: (1) the content of false teaching, (2) the core of false teaching, (3) case studies of false teaching, (4) the cure for false teaching, and (5) compassion for those affected by false teaching.

The Content of False Teaching

The significant overlap of material that Peter and Jude share in their response to false teachers might suggest that their opponents are essentially the same. A close look at each letter, however, shows important differences.[2]

Second Peter. Peter waits until the beginning of chapter 2 to acknowledge the presence of false teachers (2:1–3). Before Peter ever indicates the specific content of what the opponents believe and teach, he enumerates three things they do. First, these false teachers "secretly bring in destructive heresies, even denying the Master who bought them, bringing upon themselves swift destruction" (2:1). Before he ever specifies the content of their false teaching, Peter exposes their intentional efforts to introduce doctrines and beliefs that are out of step with the one true gospel proclaimed by the apostles and confirmed by

2 It should be noted that attempting to reconstruct the content of the false teaching based on how an author responds to it is no simple task. Scholars use a process known as "mirror-reading," which attempts to take what the biblical author says and work backward from that. It is similar to hearing one side of a phone conversation and trying to figure out what the other person is saying based only on the side of the conversation you are able to hear. One of the many challenges of mirror-reading is knowing to what extent an author is precisely recounting what the opponents are teaching or using rhetoric (e.g., exaggeration, hyperbole) to highlight the flaws of their opponents. Given the challenges of mirror-reading and the often limited information available, one must be cautious about placing too much weight on reconstructions of the specifics of false teaching and then using those reconstructions as authoritative lenses through which to interpret the biblical text. For helpful discussions of responsible mirror-reading, see John Barclay, "Mirror-Reading a Polemical Letter: Galatians as a Test Case," *JSNT* 31 (1987): 73–96; Moisés Silva, *Interpreting Galatians: Explorations in Exegetical Method*, 2nd ed. (Grand Rapids, MI: Baker, 2001), 103–12; N. K. Gupta, "Mirror-Reading Moral Issues in Paul's Letters," *JSNT* 34 (2012): 361–81; D. A. Carson, "Mirror-Reading with Paul and against Paul: Galatians 2:11–14 as a Test Case," in *Studies in the Pauline Epistles: Essays in Honor of Douglas J. Moo*, ed. Matthew S. Harmon and Jay E. Smit (Grand Rapids, MI: Zondervan, 2014), 99–112.

the Old Testament (1:16–21). Although it occurs nowhere else in the New Testament, Peter uses a Greek verb (*pareisagō*) that elsewhere describes the introduction of new beliefs or practices into a preexisting set of doctrine and practice.[3] Rather than hiding what they were teaching, the false teachers were likely "covering up the degree to which their teaching differs from the accepted apostolic teaching."[4] Second, they deny Jesus Christ as their Master. Rather than joyfully submit to his authority in their lives, these false teachers regard themselves and their desires as the final authority in their lives. Although at times they may have given the appearance of being slaves of Christ (2:20–21), their immoral sensuality demonstrates that they are slaves to their desires. Third, the false teachers are storing up eternal judgment for themselves on the last day. Their departure from the true gospel and its implications has not escaped God's notice. As Peter soberly notes, "Their condemnation from long ago is not idle, and their destruction is not asleep" (2:3).

After an extended section demonstrating from the Old Testament God's ability to rescue the godly from trials and keep the unrighteous for judgment (2:4–10a), Peter devotes the remainder of the chapter to a description of the false teachers' behavior (2:10b–22). Despite the wide-ranging, poetic nature of this description, their activities can be summarized under the three common forms of idolatry that have been common throughout human history: money, sex, and power.[5] When it comes to their obsession with money, the false teachers are no mere novices; they are "trained in greed" (2:14). Indeed, they are following in the footsteps of the greedy false prophet Balaam (2:15–16; cf. Num. 22–24). Rather than joyfully embrace God's good gift of sexuality within the parameters he has established, the false teachers

3 BDAG *pareisagō*. In Polybius it describes the attempt to introduce Carthaginian beliefs and practices into Rome (*Histories*, 6.56.12). Diodorus Siculus uses the term to describe the introduction of Egyptian ideas into Greek religious practice (*Library of History*, 1.96.5).

4 Douglas J. Moo, *2 Peter, Jude: From Biblical Text to Contemporary Life*, NIVAC (Grand Rapids, MI: Zondervan, 1996), 92.

5 See further Timothy J. Keller, *Counterfeit Gods: The Empty Promises of Money, Sex, and Power, and the Only Hope That Matters* (New York: Dutton, 2009).

enthusiastically pursue their sexual desires with little to no restraint. They have "eyes full of adultery" (2 Pet. 2:14). They use "sensual passions of the flesh" to entice others to join them in their sexual immorality (2:18). To consolidate their own power they arrogantly reject God's authority (2:1, 10–12). They use their influence to promise freedom but knowingly lead people back into slavery to their sin (2:19–22).

In the final chapter Peter finally articulates some of the false beliefs the teachers were propagating (3:1–13). In their arrogance they scoff at the promise of Christ's return (3:4). After all, they contend, things in the world have more or less continued on "as they were" since the time of the Old Testament patriarchs (3:4). Therefore, they reason, warnings and threats of final judgment can be safely disregarded. The false teachers intentionally ignore the clear teaching of Scripture that God not only created the world through water and his word, but also brought judgment on the world through water and the word at the flood (3:6), a judgment that anticipates judgment on the current heavens and earth on the last day (3:7). Rather than recognize the delay in Christ's return as an expression of God's patience leading to repentance, the false teachers see it as evidence that Christ will not in fact return (3:8–10). Rather than submit to the clear teaching of Scripture, they twist it to promote their own heretical teachings (3:16).

Jude. In contrast to 2 Peter, nowhere does Jude clearly state exactly what the opponents actually taught.[6] In fact, Jude does not

6 The identity of Jude's opponents has been long debated. A common view is that they advocate a form of Gnosticism, though advocates of this view vary in their conclusions on the extent of its developments (see the judicious discussion in Gene L. Green, *Jude and 2 Peter*, BECNT [Grand Rapids, MI: Baker Academic, 2008], 18–26). Others see the opponents as "itinerant charismatics" who emphasized their heavenly visions and participation in the heavenly realms (see, e.g., Richard Bauckham, *Jude and the Relatives of Jesus in the Early Church* [London: T&T Clark, 2004], 167). Far less likely is the conclusion that they were in fact Zealots attempting to convince Christians to participate in their rebellion against Rome in the 60s (see Herbert W. Bateman IV, *Jude*, EEC [Bellingham, WA: Lexham Press, 2017], 51–80). Some have even contended that we cannot know much of anything about the opponents because Jude uses stock language to vilify his opponents rather than in any real sense describe them (Lauri Thurén, "Hey Jude! Asking for the Original Situation and Message of a Catholic Epistle," *NTS* 43 [1997]: 451–65). Even if we cannot confidently identify the specifics of what the opponents taught, Jude

even refer to them as false teachers or false prophets. He introduces the opponents as "certain people [who] have crept in unnoticed" (4), suggesting they are outsiders. In the most basic sense they are ungodly, by which Jude means that their lives (i.e., thoughts, beliefs, emotions, inclinations, desires, actions, etc.) are not fundamentally oriented toward God but rather toward themselves. His description of judgment emphasizes their ungodliness. The Lord will judge "all the *ungodly* of all their deeds of *ungodliness* that they have committed in such an *ungodly* way, and of all the harsh things that *ungodly* sinners have spoken against him" (15). Put another way, they are "worldly people, devoid of the Spirit" (19). As a result they "pervert the grace of our God into sensuality and deny our only Master and Lord, Jesus Christ" (4). These are the two categories—perverting God's grace into sensuality and rejecting Jesus's authority—through which we can organize what the remainder of the letter says about the opponents.

Jude refers to the opponents' rejection of Jesus's authority several times. He likens them to the "the angels who did not stay within their own position of authority, but left their proper dwelling" (6). Because they rely on their dreams they reject not only Jesus's authority but all other forms of authority as well (10). In their arrogance they presume to have the authority to render judgment on spiritual beings, a kind of authority that even the archangel Michael himself does not presume to exercise because such authority belongs to the Lord (9–10). Like Korah and his followers, who rebelled against Moses in the wilderness (Num. 16:1–50), the opponents reject God's appointed leaders within the church and usurp their authority by acting as "shepherds feeding themselves" (Jude 11–12). Even the imagery Jude uses to describe the opponents highlights their rejection of authority; they are unreasoning animals (10), wild waves of the sea (13), and wandering stars (13). Nothing restrains them.

---

does give us enough of a description of their behavior to draw some basic conclusions. For a helpful and measured discussion of the issue, see Thomas R. Schreiner, *1–2 Peter and Jude*, Christian Standard Commentary (Nashville, TN: B&H, 2020), 492–99.

Because they reject the authority of Jesus as their Lord and Master, the opponents are driven by their unrestrained sinful desires. Indeed, the Greek word rendered "sensuality" (*aselgeia*) refers to a "lack of self-constraint which involves one in conduct that violates all bounds of what is socially acceptable."[7] This word regularly has sexual connotations, but Jude's use of it, while certainly including the sexual element, goes beyond to encompass other expressions of unrestrained living. Like the inhabitants of Sodom and Gomorrah, the opponents pursue various forms of sexual immorality, including the pursuit of "unnatural desire" (7). They "defile the flesh" (8), an expression that likely has connotations of sexual immorality as well.[8] Jude compares the unrestrained indulgence of their sinful desires to walking in the way of Cain (11), who, despite being warned by God that he needed to master the sin that was crouching at his door, murdered his brother Abel in a jealous rage (Gen. 4:1–16). As noted in chapter 2, later Jewish literature associated Cain with sins like greed, violence, lust, and, perhaps most relevant for Jude's context, leading others into wickedness.[9] Greed is another expression of the opponents' lack of self-control. They are like Balaam, the false prophet whom Balak king of Moab hired to curse Israel in the wilderness (Jude 11; Num. 22–24). These opponents are also unrestrained in their speech. In addition to their arrogant blasphemy of spiritual beings (Jude 8), they speak "harsh things" against the Lord himself (15). Rather than being marked by gratitude, they are grumblers (16); rather than speaking in humility to build others up, they are loud-mouthed boasters who promote themselves and their own selfish interests (16). Through their scoffing they cause division within the body of Christ (18–19).

Despite the lack of explicit statements about what Jude's opponents believed and taught, we can safely infer at least two false beliefs they

7 BDAG *aselgeia*.

8 The verb rendered "defile" (*miainō*) has the general sense of violating the purity of something, but in both the LXX (Gen. 34:5; Num. 5:14; Job 31:11) and *1 En.* 7:1 the verb clearly has a sexual sense.

9 Richard Bauckham, *Jude, 2 Peter*, WBC 50 (Dallas: Word, 1990), 79–80. See, e.g., *Jub.* 4:31; *T. Benj.* 7:1–5; *Apoc. Ab.* 24:3–5; *Apoc. Mos.* 2:1–4; 3:1–3; 40:4–5; *1 En.* 22:7.

promoted. First, they taught that because they were under God's grace they were free to live in any manner they saw fit without any fear of repercussions or judgment. Indeed, as Schreiner notes, "The most remarkable feature is the libertinism of the opponents."[10] Second, they taught that ultimate authority rested in their own direct access to the spiritual realms (primarily through dreams, 8) rather than in "the faith that was once for all delivered to the saints" (3) through "the apostles of our Lord Jesus Christ" (17).

Synthesis. Both Peter and Jude are confronted with opponents who deny the authority of Jesus Christ over them through the indulgence of their sinful passions. In both situations it seems that the opponents rejected the possibility of facing final judgment for their actions, though this is clearer in 2 Peter than in Jude. The opponents demonstrate their departure from the one true gospel proclaimed by the apostles and confirmed by the Old Testament through lives that are out of step with the moral imperatives that flow from what Jesus has done for his people. Peter is dealing with opponents who explicitly deny the return of Christ and twist Scripture; neither seems to be the case with Jude's opponents. Although more speculative, there is also likely a difference in the context in which their respective audiences live. Jude appears to have been written to believers who were familiar with Jewish traditions and noncanonical Jewish literature, whereas Peter seems to be addressing readers living in a more Greco-Roman context.

One key takeaway from both 2 Peter and Jude is the inseparable relationship between orthodoxy (right belief/doctrine) and orthopraxy (right living). In the Sermon on the Mount Jesus warned that false prophets would enter in among God's people as wolves looking to devour the sheep (Matt. 7:15–20). He gave a simple yet powerful way of identifying these false prophets and false teachers:

> You will recognize them by their fruits. Are grapes gathered from thornbushes, or figs from thistles? So, every healthy tree bears good

10 Schreiner, *1–2 Peter and Jude*, 497.

> fruit, but the diseased tree bears bad fruit. A healthy tree cannot bear bad fruit, nor can a diseased tree bear good fruit. Every tree that does not bear good fruit is cut down and thrown into the fire. Thus you will recognize them by their fruits. (Matt. 7:16–20)

Taking Jesus at his word, both Peter and Jude go to great lengths to expose the rotten fruit of their opponents as a means of inoculating the sheep from the disease that the wolves have brought with them.

The Core of False Teaching

Understanding the similarities and differences between the opponents that Peter and Jude addressed in their respective letters is an important first step. But in order to set the false teaching of these opponents within a broader biblical and theological context, we need to go back to the very beginning of the biblical story, because at the core of what Peter and Jude must confront is an error first propagated in the garden of Eden by the serpent himself. What we see there is a pattern that, at some level, all subsequent false teaching follows. That pattern has three steps.

First, false teachers question what God said. The initial sign of trouble is in the opening description of the serpent (who is later explicitly identified as Satan in Rev. 12:9) as "more crafty than any other beast of the field" (Gen. 3:1). His initial question to the woman confirms his craftiness: "Did God actually say, 'You shall not eat of any tree in the garden'?" (Gen. 3:1). There should be little doubt that Satan knew God had not prohibited eating from any tree but rather just from the tree of the knowledge of good and evil. His purpose is to raise questions and doubts about what God had actually said. Eve responds by going beyond what God had actually said: "We may eat of the fruit of the trees in the garden, but God said, 'You shall not eat of the fruit of the tree that is in the midst of the garden, neither shall you touch it, lest you die'" (Gen. 3:2–3). But a closer look at what God had actually told Adam reveals that Yahweh never prohibited *touching* the tree but only *eating* from it (Gen. 2:17). Satan has managed to muddy the waters, creating confusion as to the exact nature of what God had or had not commanded.

Second, false teachers defy or reject what God said. The serpent moves from questioning God's word to direct rejection of it in his response: "You will not surely die" (Gen. 3:4). Yahweh had been emphatic with Adam when he gave the commandment: "But of the tree of the knowledge of good and evil you shall not eat, for in the day that you eat of it you shall surely die" (Gen. 2:17). Not maybe. Not even probably. Disobedience to this one commandment would bring certain death. But Satan, emboldened by the confusion he has created in Eve's mind about the specifics of what God actually said, is now able to openly reject what God said. He is even so bold as to use the same wording that God spoke to Adam and that Eve spoke to the serpent. In effect, the serpent accuses God of lying.

Third, false teachers offer a "better" alternative by appealing to the natural appetites. The serpent explains why God actually does not want people to eat from the tree: "For God knows that when you eat of it your eyes will be opened, and you will be like God, knowing good and evil" (Gen. 3:5). Despite the fact that the man and the woman were created in the image of God, the serpent holds out the "better" alternative of determining for themselves good and evil rather than submitting to what God has already revealed as good and evil.[11] Why submit to what God says when what he has said is not true? Would it not be better to simply strike out on your own? After all, God is actually holding you back from being everything you could be. Rather than respond along the lines of "I am already like God in every way that God intends me to be, no more and no less," the woman says nothing more. Inspired by this better alternative, the woman "saw that the tree was good for food, and that it was a delight to the eyes, and that the tree was to be desired

11 When Satan says they will know good and evil, this does not mean that they will simply experience it for themselves. To know good and evil in this sense is to determine it for themselves. In contexts like this, the Hebrew verb rendered "know" (*yāda'*) occurs with the sense of discern, especially with reference to distinguishing good from evil (Deut. 1:39; Isa. 7:15). Although different Hebrew verbs are used, the same idea is present when Solomon asks for the ability as king to discern good and evil (1 Kings 3:9; cf. 1 Sam. 14:17).

to make one wise" (Gen. 3:6). Prompted by the serpent, the woman now sees the tree in a fresh light. Rather than a source of danger to be avoided at all costs, it is now an enticing path to "truly" being like God. When she stretches out her hand to touch the fruit of the tree and nothing happens, it seems as though the serpent had been right. She does not die. God must have lied to them after all.

But once Adam and Eve eat the fruit of the tree of the knowledge of good and evil, they realize that the serpent was only partially right. Their eyes are indeed opened, but rather than the promised joys of self-determination, they experience the guilt and shame of self-destruction (Gen. 3:7). Whereas before they were "naked and were not ashamed" (Gen. 2:25), now they are naked and, by implication, ashamed, as the effort to cover themselves indicates (Gen. 3:7). But their feeble efforts to cover that shame and guilt are nowhere near adequate for such a task. That shame only intensifies when Yahweh walks in the garden; rather than joyfully approaching him, they hide, knowing that they are no longer able to approach a holy God because of their disobedience (Gen. 3:8–11).

We see this same pattern in Jesus's encounter with Satan in the wilderness (Matt. 4:1–13). Right before the Holy Spirit leads him into the wilderness to be tempted, Jesus was baptized by John the Baptist. After the Spirit descends upon Jesus, God the Father declares from heaven, "This is my beloved Son, with whom I am well pleased" (Matt. 3:17). Like he did with Eve in the garden, Satan begins his temptation by questioning what God said: "If you are the Son of God, command these stones to become loaves of bread" (Matt. 4:3). While he was successful in raising doubts about God's word with Eve, the tempter is unsuccessful in his efforts to do so with Jesus. Nonetheless, Satan moves on to reject what God says, though in a more subtle manner than he did with Eve. Continuing in his efforts to question what God said, Satan takes Jesus to the pinnacle and says, "If you are the Son of God, throw yourself down, for it is written, 'He will command his angels concerning you,' and 'On their hands they will bear you up, lest you strike your foot against a stone'" (Matt. 4:6, citing Ps. 91:11–12). On the surface, quoting Psalm 91:11–12 might seem like Satan is embracing God's word. But by intentionally twisting and misapplying it, he is in fact rejecting its authority by trying to make it mean something that it does not. In his final temptation of Jesus, Satan proposes a "better" alternative to receiving universal dominion than the long path of obedience and the suffering it will entail. He offers Jesus all the kingdoms of the world if he will simply fall down before Satan and worship him (Matt. 4:8–9). But rather than choose the path of least resistance, Jesus rejects Satan's offer and reaffirms his loyalty to the Father (Matt. 4:10–11). At every point where Adam and Eve had failed to resist the wiles of the serpent, Jesus obeyed!

Each aspect of this pattern is also present in 2 Peter, though not always in the most obvious way. Peter refers to the "the ignorant and unstable" who twist Scripture to their own destruction (2 Pet. 3:16). One obvious form of twisting Scripture is calling into question what God has said. Peter's opponents ask the question, "Where is the promise of his coming?" (3:4). Despite the explicit promise of the Lord Jesus that he would return for his people (e.g., John 14:1–4), the opponents question whether he said it or perhaps whether he meant it.

From this posture of questioning God's word they move to a direct rejection of what Jesus said. They do so based on their own brand of flawed logic: "For ever since the fathers fell asleep, all things are continuing as they were from the beginning of creation" (2 Pet. 3:4). The return of Christ is not possible, according to the opponents, because the world has remained the same since the days of Israel's patriarchs. But their rejection of God's word is most evident in their rejection of God's moral standards, which have been clearly revealed in the Old Testament and reaffirmed by the apostles of Jesus (3:1–3). They casually dismiss God's condemnation of greed (Ex. 20:17), sexual immorality (Ex. 20:14), rebellion against authority (Num. 16:50), pride/arrogance (Prov. 3:34), and impurity (Ps. 24:3–4).

Having questioned and then rejected God's word, Peter's opponents seek to offer a better alternative to faithfulness to God by appealing to a variety of appetites. Most noticeably they appeal to the seemingly unrestrained expression of sexual desire, described in various ways as sensuality (2 Pet. 2:2, 7, 18), indulging the lusts of defiling passions (2:10), and eyes full of adultery (2:14). Indeed, they actively "entice by sensual passions of the flesh those who are barely escaping from those who live in error" (2:18). They appeal to the desire for autonomy, offering freedom when they are in fact leading people into slavery to corruption (2:19).

While not as evident in Jude, hints of this pattern are still present. His opponents "pervert the grace of our God into sensuality" (Jude 4), language that could reflect either their questioning of God's word spoken through the apostles or their rejection of it. They "deny our only Master and Lord, Jesus Christ" (4), which at some level must include a rejection of what he taught. These opponents clearly reject God's revealed moral commands with regard to sexuality (6–7, 16, 18), submitting to God's appointed leaders (8–11), and greed (11), among other areas. Although Jude does not explicitly say so, these opponents are clearly using their wiles to appeal to people within the body of Christ, trying to entice them to embrace their rejection of God's moral standards and embrace their sinful desires.

Case Studies of False Teaching

Peter and Jude are not content to merely identify the errors of their opponents. They use case studies of false teaching from redemptive history to help their readers understand their experience with the opponents. Although in some instances the Old Testament itself does not connect false teaching with the specific figures mentioned by Peter and Jude, oftentimes noncanonical Jewish literature did make that association.

As noted before, the angels who sinned by abandoning their appointed boundaries refers to Genesis 6:1–4, where the "sons of God" took the "daughters of men" as wives and produced offspring (see 2 Pet. 2:4; Jude 6). Jewish literature, and in particular *1 Enoch*, expanded upon this cryptic story, referring to these rebellious angels as "watchers." These watchers were responsible for teaching humanity various magic arts, revealing various forms of technology (e.g., making of weaponry, knowledge about plants, incantations, etc.) as well as encouraging corrupt and immoral behaviors (*1 En.* 7–8). As a result Enoch, who had been taken to heaven without dying (Gen. 5:24), is sent to announce God's judgment on the watchers (*1 En.* 12:1–13:1). Both Peter and Jude describe the events of Genesis 6:1–4 in a way that suggests their audiences were familiar with not only the biblical account but also the Jewish traditions surrounding it. As such, these rebellious angels are a case study in leading people away from God through both their teaching and their conduct.

Balaam is another case study that Peter and Jude use. Whereas Jude simply refers to "Balaam's error" (Jude 11), Peter elaborates further. The opponents "have followed the way of Balaam" who "loved gain from wrongdoing" (2 Pet. 2:15). Balak, king of Moab, enticed Balaam to speak a curse on God's people in the name of Yahweh (Num. 22–24). When God thwarted Balak by speaking a blessing over Israel through Balaam, Balaam encouraged Balak to tempt Israel to commit idolatry by enticing them through sexual immorality (Num. 31:16). Therefore Balaam became a symbol for putting stumbling blocks in the path of God's people (Deut. 23:5–6; Josh. 13:22; 24:9; Neh. 13:2; Mic. 6:5; Jude 11; Rev. 2:14). Later Jewish literature highlighted Balaam's prevarication, greed, and sexual immorality,[12] a backdrop that may inform Peter and Jude's use of the Balaam story here.

Jude uses two additional case studies not found in 2 Peter. The first is that of Cain; Jude simply asserts that the opponents "walked in the way of Cain" (Jude 11) without elaborating further. Genesis 4 records Cain's murder of his brother Abel and subsequent banishment, a stark warning of the dangers that hatred can produce. But as we have already noted, Jewish literature linked Cain to greed and leading others into wickedness. Thus Jude appears to see in Cain a picture of the opponents, who because they are motivated by greed and lust attempt to lead others astray. The second is Korah, who led a

12 See the helpful discussions in Bauckham, *Jude, 2 Peter*, 81–83; and Peter H. Davids, *The Letters of 2 Peter and Jude*, PNTC (Grand Rapids, MI: Eerdmans, 2006), 253–56.

rebellion against Moses in the wilderness (Num. 16:1–50). In addition to his obvious rejection of God and his appointed leaders, later Jewish writings associated Korah with a rejection of the divine authority of the Mosaic law. Indeed, according to Richard Bauckham, Korah "became the classic example of the antinomian heretic."[13] This tradition appears to have been picked up by the early Christians, which may explain how Jude can simply mention Korah's rebellion without further elaboration. Thus Jude sees in his opponents the reflection of Korah as they reject God's appointed leaders in the church and the divine authority of God's moral law.

The Cure for False Teaching

Identifying the nature of what the opponents taught and how they lived is a necessary step to dealing with it rightly. But by itself it is insufficient. Both Peter and Jude recognize that believers must be firmly grounded in the truth of the gospel. Knowing the true gospel inside and out is a crucial way of being able to identify departures from the gospel and remain true to Jesus. What unites believers is their "common salvation" experienced through knowing Jesus, a faith "that was once for all delivered to the saints" (Jude 3). Yet the truth of this gospel is something that believers must "contend for" like athletes competing in the arena (3). "The struggle of Christian living is a contest on behalf of the gospel, not in the sense of merely *defending* the gospel against attacks, but in the offensive sense of positively promoting the advance and victory of the gospel in human life."[14] To help believers resist the wiles of the opponents, Peter and Jude highlight several different aspects of the gospel.

First, they highlight the true identity of Jesus. Peter reminds believers that Jesus shares in the honor and glory of God the Father because he is the beloved Son in whom he delights (2 Pet. 1:16–18), a reality

13 Bauckham, *Jude, 2 Peter*, 83. He notes the following texts: *L.A.B.* 16:1; *Tg. Ps.-J.* on Num. 16; *Num. Rab.* 18:3.

14 Richard Bauckham, *2 Peter, Jude*, Word Biblical Themes (Dallas: Word, 1990), 21; emphasis original.

anticipated in the Old Testament Scriptures and witnessed firsthand by Peter and the apostles (1:16–21). Central to Jesus's identity is that he is our Savior (2 Pet. 1:1, 11; 2:20; 3:2, 18; Jude 5, 25). Just as he saved the Israelites from their bondage in Egypt (Jude 5), Jesus has now redeemed his people from their bondage to sin (2 Pet. 2:1). But Jesus is more than simply a Savior; he is also our "Master and Lord" (Jude 4). He has complete and final authority not only over creation in some generalized sense, but in particular over his people (2 Pet. 2:1). At the end of human history he will consummate his eternal kingdom in a new creation where righteousness dwells (1:11; 3:11–13). Therefore, because Jesus is our Master, Lord, and Savior, those who claim to be his people must resist those who deny his authority either directly through their teaching or indirectly through their indulgence of sinful desires.

Second, Peter highlights the cleansing from sin that believers experience through the gospel. Through the gospel believers have already "escaped from the corruption that is in the world because of sinful desire" (1:4). When believers put their initial trust in Jesus, they are united to Christ and "become partakers of the divine nature" (1:4). Through the promises of the gospel the Spirit begins to transform the believer to more clearly reflect Jesus Christ (Rom. 8:28–30), who is the image of God (Heb. 1:3). Indeed, failure to pursue spiritual growth in the areas of faith, virtue, knowledge, self-control, etc. (2 Pet. 1:5–7) is evidence that people have forgotten that at their conversion they were "cleansed from [their] former sins" (1:9). Peter returns to this initial cleansing from sin when he notes that if, "after they have escaped the defilements of the world through the knowledge of our Lord and Savior Jesus Christ, they are again entangled in them and overcome, the last state has become worse for them than the first" (2:20).

Third, the gospel gives believers the power to obey in the present. Because believers know the Lord and his power in their lives, they have everything necessary for life and godliness (1:3). This knowledge of the Lord is experienced through "his precious and very great promises" that make us "partakers of the divine nature" and have freed us from the corruption of the world and its sinful desires (1:4). These promises enable the believer to "supplement" their faith with growth in different character qualities that reflect Jesus (1:5–8). As they pursue these qualities, believers will confirm that before the foundation of the world God chose them and has called them to be his own (1:10). Believers are able to live "lives of holiness and godliness" as they eagerly wait for Christ to return (3:11–12). Because believers have the Spirit of God, they are able to build up their faith and pray in the power of the Spirit (Jude 20).

Lastly, the gospel gives believers hope for the future. Jesus will grant his people entrance into his eternal kingdom (2 Pet. 1:11). When the day of the Lord arrives like a thief in the night, believers will be ushered into a "new heavens and a new earth in which righteousness dwells" (3:13). On that day believers will receive "the mercy of our Lord Jesus Christ that leads to eternal life" (Jude 21). The Lord Jesus will present his people "blameless before the presence of his glory with great joy" (24). It is that hope that empowers believers to resist the false promises of the opponents and remain true to the gospel proclaimed by the apostles of the Lord Jesus Christ.

Compassion for Those Affected by False Teaching

Despite the strong language directed at the false teachers, Jude is not ready to write off those who have been deceived by them. He distinguishes three different categories of people and prescribes a specific approach for each group (Jude 22–23).[15]

First, Jude exhorts believers to "have mercy on those who doubt" (22). Because God is merciful (Ex. 34:6–7; Ps. 116:5) and believers have set their hope on the mercy they will receive when Christ returns (Jude 21), they should be people who themselves extend mercy to others. While the expression "those who doubt" could also be rendered

15 Determining the original wording of verses 22–23 is difficult because of the diversity within the earliest manuscripts; for helpful discussions of the variants, see Tommy Wasserman, *The Epistle of Jude: Its Text and Transmission*, ConBNT 43 (Stockholm, SE: Almqvist & Wiksell, 2006), 320–29; and Bateman, *Jude*, 370–75.

"those who dispute," the context indicates Jude likely has in mind those who doubt or waver in their faith.[16] The persuasive abilities of the false teachers and their appeal to the natural appetites can cause people to waver in their faith. But rather than condemn such people for their lack of faith, believers should show them mercy.

Second, believers should "save others by snatching them out of the fire" (23). This second group of individuals seems to have moved beyond wavering to embracing at least some of the false teachers' beliefs and practices. The promised fires of eternal judgment (7) are pictured as surrounding them. As a result, believers must take decisive action to snatch such people from the fiery judgment that awaits those who abandon the true gospel for the lies of the false teachers.

Finally, for the last group of individuals believers should "show mercy with fear, hating even the garment stained by the flesh" (23). Even those who are deeply ensnared by sin because they have followed the false teachers should be approached with mercy. Yet this mercy must not be naïve; it must be accompanied by fear that one might fall into the same sin (Gal. 6:1) and a hatred for the sin that has corrupted their lives. Pursuing such a difficult course of action is possible only because God himself shows his people mercy while at the same time remaining perfectly pure and holy.

Jude draws his language and imagery from Zechariah 3:1–8. The postexilic prophet has a vision of the high priest Joshua standing in the presence of the Lord "clothed with filthy garments" (Zech. 3:3). Satan stands there as well, accusing Joshua (Zech. 3:1). The Lord rebukes Satan (Zech. 3:2) and clothes Joshua with "pure vestments" (Zech. 3:4) and a "clean turban" (Zech. 3:5) to visually demonstrate that God has taken away his iniquity (Zech. 3:4). As a result, God refers to Joshua as "a brand plucked from the fire" (Zech. 3:2). Jude sees in this a picture of what can happen for those who turn away from the lies of the false teachers and return to the true gospel of the Lord Jesus Christ.

16 The same verb (*diakrinō*) is used in verse 9 to describe Michael disputing with Satan over the body of Moses; see discussion in Schreiner, *1–2 Peter and Jude*, 590–91.

Conclusion

In the week leading up to his death, Jesus had warned his followers that opponents of the gospel would arise and seek to mislead them (Matt. 24:23–28). Peter and Jude use their pastoral wisdom and robust understanding of the true gospel to expose the false teaching and immoral lives of the opponents. The need to be vigilant in the face of false teaching will remain a perpetual need for the church until Christ returns. But the good news is that the gospel is sufficient for life and godliness as we wait with eager anticipation for our Lord to return and consummate the new creation where "nothing unclean will ever enter it, nor anyone who does what is detestable or false, but only those who are written in the Lamb's book of life" (Rev. 21:27).

4

God's Preservation of His Persevering People

SCRIPTURE REGULARLY PLACES TRUTHS side by side that on the surface can seem to be in tension with each other. A classic example is Pharaoh's hardened heart. On the one hand there are several statements that Pharaoh hardened his own heart in response to Yahweh's demand that he let his people Israel go (e.g., Ex. 8:15, 32; 9:34). On the other hand, there are statements where God himself is said to harden Pharaoh's heart (e.g., Ex. 4:21; 7:3; 9:12). Another example is divine sovereignty and human responsibility. In his Pentecost sermon, Peter asserts that "this Jesus, delivered up according to the definite plan and foreknowledge of God, you crucified and killed by the hands of lawless men" (Acts 2:23). The crucifixion of Jesus was God's sovereign plan all along, yet those who executed him were responsible for their actions.

A similar dynamic is present in 2 Peter and Jude when it comes to the twin themes of God preserving his people until the end and his people persevering in the faith until the end. On the one hand, both authors stress God's ability and intention to preserve his people so that they will inherit what he has promised them. On the other hand, Jude and Peter remind believers that they must persevere in the faith until the end if they are going to enter the eternal kingdom of the Lord Jesus Christ.

The God Who Preserves His People

All throughout the Old Testament God demonstrates his power and ability to preserve his people. On the corporate level, this is seen most clearly in Israel's wilderness wandering. As Israel sat on the plains of Moab preparing to enter the promised land, Moses knew that it would be important for that generation of Israelites to understand and remember what God had already done for them. Therefore, throughout Deuteronomy, God uses Moses to remind the people of the ways that he preserved them the past forty years as they wandered in the wilderness. In the most basic sense God preserved his people by providing for their basic physical needs. As a prelude to renewing the covenant with Israel, God reminds the people:

> I have led you forty years in the wilderness. Your clothes have not worn out on you, and your sandals have not worn off your feet. You have not eaten bread, and you have not drunk wine or strong drink, that you may know that I am the LORD your God. (Deut. 29:5–6; cf. 8:4; Neh. 9:21)

Six days a week God provided manna for the people (Ex. 16:1–36). Several times he provided water for them in miraculous ways (Ex. 17:1–7; Num. 20:2–13). Despite the harsh conditions of the wilderness their clothes and sandals did not wear out. God showed his power to preserve his people by providing for their physical needs even in harsh wilderness conditions.

God also preserved his people in the midst of threats from other nations. Beginning with Yahweh's decisive drowning of the Egyptian army in the Red Sea (Ex. 14:26–31), God preserved his people by fighting for them. When the Amalekites attacked them on the way to Sinai (Ex. 17:8–16), God preserved them. During their forty years in the wilderness, God preserved his people in the face of numerous enemies, including Arad (Num. 21:1–2), Sihon king of the Amorites (Num. 21:21–30), Og king of Bashan (Num. 21:31–35), and the Midianites (Num. 31:1–54).

Lastly, and perhaps most relevant for Jude and 2 Peter, God also preserved his people in the face of false teaching and false worship. After Israel and Aaron committed idolatry by making the golden calf (Ex. 32:1–6), Moses pleaded with God to preserve his people despite their unfaithfulness (Ex. 32:7–14; 32:31–33:23). God renewed his covenant with those who repented and reassured his people of his presence with them as they journeyed to the promised land (Ex. 33:12–17; 34:10–28). In the face of opposition to Moses's leadership (Num. 12:1–16; 16:1–50), God purged his people in order to preserve a faithful remnant of his people. When Balak king of Moab bribed the false prophet Balaam to pronounce a curse upon Israel, God instead used him to pronounce a series of blessings upon them (Num. 22–24). In response to some within Israel committing idolatry with the daughters of Moab, God preserved his people by instructing Moses to hang all the chiefs of Israel for their unfaithfulness (Num. 25:1–18). Time after time God preserved his people on their way to the promised land. This reality was so important for Israel to understand that he embedded it within the blessing that the high priest spoke over the people in worship: "The Lord bless you and keep you; the Lord make his face to shine upon you and be gracious to you; the Lord lift up his countenance upon you and give you peace" (Num. 6:24–26).

One passage that succinctly brings together these three distinct ways God preserved his people in their wilderness wanderings is Joshua 24. In response to Joshua's challenge to remain faithful to Yahweh, the people respond:

> Far be it from us that we should forsake the Lord to serve other gods, for it is the Lord our God who brought us and our fathers up from the land of Egypt, out of the house of slavery, and who did those great signs in our sight and preserved us in all the way that we went, and among all the peoples through whom we passed. And the Lord drove out before us all the peoples, the Amorites who lived in the land. Therefore we also will serve the Lord, for he is our God. (Josh. 24:16–18)

God's preservation of his people throughout their wilderness wandering and conquest of the land is the basis for Joshua's call for Israel to renew their exclusive commitment to serving Yahweh.

That preservation of his people continues throughout the Old Testament. When the prophet Elijah complains that he is the only faithful follower of Yahweh in all Israel (1 Kings 19:14), God asserts that he has preserved a remnant of seven thousand who have not bowed the knee to Baal (1 Kings 19:18; cf. Rom. 11:4). As part of his mission the messianic servant of Yahweh will "bring back the preserved of Israel" (Isa. 49:6). Micah 2:12 anticipates a day when God "will gather the remnant of Israel" as part of his redemptive plan. Isaiah 10:20–22 expands on this promise, noting that a remnant of God's people will return to him and lean on him rather than on false gods and corrupt leaders. Over the centuries God has repeatedly demonstrated his power and willingness to preserve his people, even despite their sin.

In addition to God's preservation of his people on a corporate level, the Old Testament shows numerous examples of God preserving individuals from danger, whether physical or spiritual. Faced with the threat of a fiery death if they did not bow down in worship to Nebuchadnezzar's golden image, God preserved Shadrach, Meshach, and Abednego in the midst of the fiery furnace (Dan. 3:1–30). The psalms are filled with prayers for God to preserve individuals and examples of God doing just that. David regularly prays for God to preserve him in the face of enemies or difficult circumstances (Pss. 16:1; 25:20; 59:1; 86:2; 140:4). Alongside those requests for God to keep or preserve his people are repeated assertions that he has done so and will continue to do so (Pss. 31:23; 32:7; 34:20; 37:28; 40:11; 41:2; 86:2; 91:11; 97:10; 116:6; 121:1–8; 138:7; 143:11; 145:20). Psalm 121 is a particularly good example. Notice the repeated references to God "keeping" his people:

> I lift up my eyes to the hills.
>
> From where does my help come?

My help comes from the LORD,
who made heaven and earth.

He will not let your foot be moved;
he who *keeps* you will not slumber.
Behold, he who *keeps* Israel
will neither slumber nor sleep.

The LORD is your *keeper*;
the LORD is your shade on your right hand.
The sun shall not strike you by day,
nor the moon by night.

The LORD will *keep* you from all evil;
he will *keep* your life.
The LORD will *keep* your going out and your coming in
from this time forth and forevermore.

The Lord's power and ability to keep his people even in the midst of all life's circumstances is a pillar of the Old Testament hope.

Thus it should come as no surprise that both Jude and 2 Peter draw on this rich heritage as a means of encouraging their readers of God's power to preserve them until the end. Indeed, God's power to keep his people is a central theme in Jude. He begins by addressing his recipients as "those who are called, beloved in God the Father and *kept for Jesus Christ*" (Jude 1). Another way of translating the italicized phrase is "kept by Jesus Christ" (see ESV mg.), in which case the point would be that Jesus Christ is the one who keeps his people. Either way, the passive voice of the verb "kept" indicates that someone (either God the Father or Jesus Christ) is preserving his people. That sets the stage for Jude's lengthy warning about the false teachers threatening the church (3–19).

Jude returns to this theme of God's power to keep his people in the concluding benediction. He writes:

> Now to him who is able to *keep* you from stumbling and to present you blameless before the presence of his glory with great joy, to the only God, our Savior, through Jesus Christ our Lord, be glory, majesty, dominion, and authority, before all time and now and forever. Amen. (24–25)

God's power extends to preserving his people from "stumbling," a word that describes falling into the immorality, rebellion, and apostasy of the false teachers. Because God is able to keep his people from stumbling so as not to abandon their faith in Jesus, he is also able to present his people blameless before himself on the last day with great joy. By placing references to God's ability to keep his people at the beginning and the end of the letter, Jude frames the entirety of his letter within the comfort and stability that come from that truth.

This same theme is present in 2 Peter, although with slightly different terminology. In 2 Peter 2:4–10 Peter notes several Old Testament examples of God bringing judgment on those who rebelled against his appointed boundaries. Along with those negative examples, Peter highlights God's preservation of two individuals. In contrast to the ancient world destroyed by the flood, God "preserved Noah, a herald of righteousness" (2:5). From the midst of wicked Sodom and Gomorrah God "rescued righteous Lot" (2:7). "As models for his readers, the author seems to have deliberately chosen righteous men in worst-case situations, living almost alone in flagrantly unjust societies, standing for righteousness in situations where wickedness seemed wholly triumphant."[1] These examples culminate in Peter's thesis statement that "the Lord knows how to rescue the godly from trials, and to keep the unrighteous under punishment until the day of judgment" (2:9). Since God has given everything necessary for life and godliness through his great promises (1:3–4), it makes sense that he would preserve his people through even the most difficult of circumstances, including threats from the apostate false teachers. Indeed, in 1 Peter 1:5 the apostle asserts that believers "by God's power are being guarded through faith for a salvation ready to be revealed in the last time."

1 Richard Bauckham, *2 Peter, Jude*, Word Biblical Themes (Dallas: Word, 1990), 64.

In highlighting God's power to preserve his people, both Jude and Peter are in line with what Jesus himself said on the night he was betrayed. While praying with his disciples, Jesus says:

> Holy Father, keep them in your name, which you have given me, that they may be one, even as we are one. While I was with them, I kept them in your name, which you have given me. I have guarded them, and not one of them has been lost except the son of destruction, that the Scripture might be fulfilled. (John 17:11–12)

God's power to preserve his people even in the face of threats from false teachers and our own sinful tendencies is a constant source of comfort and encouragement for believers.

The Perseverance of God's People

Right alongside the emphasis on God's power to preserve his people, both Peter and Jude also emphasize the necessity of God's people persevering in their faith to the end. In doing so they are tapping into an important Old Testament theme.

An obvious example is Caleb, one of the twelve spies sent to spy out the promised land (Num. 13–14). When they reported back, they described not only the abundant fruitfulness of the land but also the intimidating strength of the inhabitants (Num. 13:25–29). But rather than focus on either the goodness of the land or the strength of its inhabitants, Caleb (along with Joshua) urged the people to "go up at once and occupy it, for we are well able to overcome it" (Num. 13:30). Together they reminded the people:

> If the Lord delights in us, he will bring us into this land and give it to us, a land that flows with milk and honey. Only do not rebel against the Lord. And do not fear the people of the land, for they are bread for us. Their protection is removed from them, and the Lord is with us; do not fear them. (Num. 14:8–9)

When God announces that Israel will spend the next forty years wandering in the wilderness as judgment for their rebellion (Num. 14:20–38), he exempts Caleb "because he has a different spirit and has followed me fully" and promises, "I will bring [him] into the land into which he went, and his descendants shall possess it" (Num. 14:24)

For the next forty years Caleb wanders in the wilderness, continuing to trust in Yahweh and his promises as he watches the rebellious generation of Israelites die off. It is not until five years into the conquest of the land that Caleb finally asks for his inheritance (Josh. 14:6–15). He asserts that he has "wholly followed the LORD my God" (Josh. 14:8–9). God has preserved his life (Josh. 14:10), and his strength has in no way waned despite his being eighty-five years old (Josh. 14:11). Despite the presence of the Anakim in the land he requests, Caleb remains resolute in his faith in Yahweh: "It may be that the LORD will be with me, and I shall drive them out just as the LORD said" (Josh. 14:12). As a result "Hebron became the inheritance of Caleb the son of Jephunneh the Kenizzite to this day, because he wholly followed the LORD, the God of Israel" (Josh. 14:14). Caleb is a model of faith that perseveres until the end and receives the promises of God.

Psalm 95 also uses Israel's experience in the wilderness to call for persevering faith. The first half of the psalm calls God's people to worship him with joyful exuberance (Ps. 95:1–7). The second half of the psalm issues a stark warning about the dangers of failing to persevere in the faith (Ps. 95:8–11). God's people must not "harden their hearts" like Israel did in the wilderness at Meribah/Massah (see Ex. 17:1–7) by putting him to the test (Ps. 95:8–10). God "loathed that generation" during their forty years in the wilderness because they went astray in their hearts (Ps. 95:10). As a result they were not able to enter God's rest in the promised land (Ps. 95:11). Their failure to persevere in faith led to their destruction.

It is against this backdrop that both Jude and Peter exhort their readers to persevere in their faith in the true gospel. From start to finish Jude makes persevering in the faith a key emphasis. His purpose for writing is to appeal to them "to contend for the faith that was once for all delivered to the saints" (Jude 3). By using a verb from the realm of athletic competition Jude presents the Christian life as a continual fight to maintain one's fidelity to the Lord. Jewish writers used similar language to depict "the struggle which the pious has to go through in this world."[2] Believers must make intentional effort to remain true to the gospel that has been handed down to them through the apostles because false teachers seek to pervert that gospel into a license for pursuing their own sinful desires (Jude 3–4).

To support his call for the necessity of persevering in the faith, Jude uses a series of Old Testament and Second Temple Jewish examples. The first one is paradigmatic for the rest:

> Now I want to remind you, although you once fully knew it, that Jesus, who saved a people out of the land of Egypt, afterward destroyed those who did not believe. (5)

Jude stresses that what he says is something his readers already knew but needed to be reminded of. That truth is that not everyone whom Jesus saved from Egypt made it to the promised land. Those who did not believe were destroyed. For some it was their idolatry with the golden calf (Ex. 32–34); for others it was their refusal to enter the promised land when commanded to do so (Num. 13–14). Still others fell in the wilderness for various acts of idolatry or rebellion (e.g., Num. 16:1–50; 25:1–17). The point is that only those who, like Caleb (Num. 14:24), continued to trust in Yahweh were able to enter the promised land. In the same way, Jude's audience must remember and believe "the predictions of the apostles of our Lord Jesus Christ" (Jude 17) if they are to receive mercy from him at his return (21).

That foundation sets the stage for Jude's central command related to persevering in the Christian life. He writes:

2 *TDNT* 1:135; cf. 4 Macc. 16:16; 17:13–14; Philo, *Agr.* 111–18.

> But you, beloved, building yourselves up in your most holy faith and praying in the Holy Spirit, keep yourselves in the love of God, waiting for the mercy of our Lord Jesus Christ that leads to eternal life. (20–21)

The heart of this lengthy sentence is the command to "keep yourselves in the love of God" (21). Grammatically the phrase "love of God" could refer either to God's love for the believer or the believer's love for God. While the two are inseparably connected (our love for God depends on God's prior love for us; 1 John 4:7–12), the emphasis likely falls on God's love for us. Jude opened the letter by referring to believers as "beloved in God the Father" (Jude 1). God's love is pictured as a realm or area that believers must actively seek to remain within.

Jude gives three ways that believers keep themselves in God's love.[3] The first is "building yourselves up in your most holy faith" (20). Jude's language portrays the believer building upon an already existing foundation rather than starting from scratch.[4] In the New Testament, building language is regularly associated with the picture of God's people as a temple for his people to dwell in (cf. Eph. 2:19–22; 1 Pet. 2:4–8). Although each individual believer is responsible to pursue his/her own growth in the faith, the emphasis here is on believers cooperating together to enhance the spiritual health of the entire community of believers. "If they build on the foundation of their *holy* faith, then the community they build will be a holy one, living out the moral requirements of the gospel."[5] The true faith once for all delivered to the saints sets believers apart and produces a life of holiness (cf. 2 Pet. 1:5–8). Such a community built on a holy faith will reject the immoral lifestyle promoted by the false teachers and in doing so remain secure in the realm of God's love for them.

3 Each of these three ways is expressed by a present-tense participle, portraying the action as continuous.

4 The verb *epoikodomeō* means "to build something on something already built" (BDAG *epoikodomeō* [2]).

5 Bauckham, *2 Peter, Jude*, 23; emphasis original.

The second way that believers keep themselves in God's love is by "praying in the Holy Spirit" (Jude 20). In contrast to the false teachers who are devoid of the Spirit (19), believers are able to pray continuously in the power and guidance of the Holy Spirit (cf. Eph. 6:18). As the temple of God's presence, believers are indwelt by the Spirit, both individually and corporately. Believers have a "most holy faith" and are being built into a holy place (i.e., a temple) so that God's Holy Spirit can live within them. Believers pray because they want to experience intimacy with a holy God, and the Holy Spirit facilitates that connection by empowering our prayers and interceding on our behalf (Rom. 8:26). Whereas the false teachers rely on claims of visions and prophecies to ground their immorality, true believers rely on the power and guidance of the Holy Spirit to empower holy lives that keep them secure in the realm of God's love.

The final way that believers keep themselves in God's love is by "waiting for the mercy of our Lord Jesus Christ that leads to eternal life" (Jude 21). The specific verb Jude uses regularly has an eschatological sense as it does here (cf. Mark 15:43; Luke 23:51; Titus 2:13).[6] This is not a passive waiting, but an eager expectation that produces a life of holiness. What believers set their hope upon is the mercy that Jesus Christ will show them, which is in sharp contrast to the terrifying judgment awaiting the false teachers (Jude 14–16). That mercy is experienced through the true gospel taught by the apostles (3, 17) and is rooted in the substitutionary death of Jesus for his people and his resurrection from the dead (Rom. 3:21–26). The mercy that Jude prayed would be multiplied in the present (Jude 2) is at the same time the object of the believer's future hope. Such mercy leads to eternal life with God, experiencing the fullness of his presence and living as redeemed image bearers in a new creation. Believers pursue a life of holiness as an expression of their hope in Jesus's mercy, not as a means to earn it.

Embedded within these key verses are two triads that were central to the early church. The first is the Trinitarian shape of Jude's exhortation.

6 BDAG *prosdechomai* (2).

Although it is not explicit, the context indicates that God in the phrase "love of God" refers to the Father (21), since Jude began his letter by describing believers as "beloved in God the Father" (1). The mercy that believers wait for comes from the Lord Jesus Christ (21). The prayers of believers are empowered and guided by the Holy Spirit (20). It is this nascent Trinitarianism that eventually led the church to affirm there is one God who exists in three equal persons.

The second triad is faith, hope, and love. Although it is more famous for its appearance in Paul's letters (e.g., 1 Cor. 13:13; Col. 1:4–5; 1 Thess. 5:8), Jude expresses it too, albeit with slightly different language. Believers must pursue growth in their "most holy faith" (Jude 20). As recipients of God's love (1) they must keep themselves in that love (21). They do so by waiting for (i.e., eagerly anticipating and setting their hope upon) the mercy of Jesus when he returns. Again it should be noted that Jude envisions keeping ourselves in God's love as a community project. Believers, "by their solidarity with one another, their submission to Jesus as Lord, and their care for their erring brothers and sisters, display community-building virtues."[7]

Each believer is responsible to play his or her part in pursuing not only personal spiritual growth but also the spiritual growth of fellow believers. That requires intentional involvement in the church that goes beyond merely attending a weekly worship service. It requires intentionally building relationships with fellow believers that enable us to know when others are struggling or tempted to walk away from the faith.

Although less of an emphasis in 2 Peter, the apostle still addresses the necessity of believers persevering in the faith until the end. Based on what God has done for us through the gospel (2 Pet. 1:3–4), Peter commands believers to diligently pursue growth in various character qualities that mark a genuine believer (1:3–9). Practicing these qualities ensures that a person will never fall away from the faith (1:10) and

7 Peter H. Davids, *A Theology of James, Peter, and Jude*, BTNT 6 (Grand Rapids, MI: Zondervan, 2014), 292.

guarantees entrance into Christ's kingdom on the last day (1:11). Peter's purpose in writing this letter is to provide a reminder of the need to persevere in the true gospel (1:12–15; 3:1), so that even long after his death believers "may be able at any time to recall these things" (1:15).

Within the series of Old Testament examples that demonstrate God's ability to "rescue the godly from trials, and to keep the unrighteous under punishment until the day of judgment" (2:9), Peter highlights two men who demonstrated persevering in the faith despite difficult circumstances. The first is Noah, whom he describes as a "herald of righteousness" (2:5). Building such an enormous boat would have taken many years, during which time Noah, as a righteous man (Gen. 6:8–9), would have had to persevere in believing what God had revealed to him while living in the midst of wicked people. By calling Noah a herald of righteousness Peter seems to imply that he also proclaimed the coming judgment of God and invited the wicked to repent of their ways before it was too late. The second example is Lot, a "righteous man" who was "tormenting his righteous soul" day and night because of the wickedness around him (2 Pet. 2:8). His perseverance is put forward as a model for Peter's readers as they must endure the lies and immorality of the false teachers.

The apostle returns to the theme of perseverance as he closes the letter. Because believers are waiting for the new creation where righteousness dwells (3:13), they must "be diligent to be found by him without spot or blemish, and at peace" (3:14). This same diligence directed toward pursuing growth in godly character qualities to confirm one's calling and election (1:10) is mentioned again in an effort to motivate believers to a life of purity. Believers must pursue being without spot or blemish because they follow a Savior who was "a lamb without blemish or spot" (1 Pet. 1:19). Just as sacrifices under the Mosaic covenant had to be without blemish (e.g., Lev. 1:3, 10; 3:1, etc.), so too the lives of God's people should be offered as sacrifices that are without blemish. The pursuit of spiritual growth also has the practical effect of providing stability in order to persevere in the true gospel in the face of opposition from false teachers and the temptations of the flesh (2 Pet. 3:18).

Conclusion

God preserves his people. God's people must persevere in their faith. Jude and Peter affirm both of these truths simultaneously, without offering an explicit explanation of how those two realities work in conjunction with each other. In doing so they follow in the footsteps of other biblical authors. Psalm 91:14–16 is an excellent example:

> Because he holds fast to me in love, I will deliver him;
> I will protect him, because he knows my name.
> When he calls to me, I will answer him;
> I will be with him in trouble;
> I will rescue him and honor him.
> With long life I will satisfy him
> and show him my salvation.

God empowers his people to persevere in the faith and in doing so preserves them faithful until the end. Our perseverance is motivated by the comfort that comes from knowing that God will preserve us as we continue to put our trust in him.

5

The New Heavens and the New Earth

"AND THEY ALL LIVED HAPPILY EVER AFTER." That's the ending to a lot of the stories we heard as children. But as we get older, we realize how rarely that happens in the "real world." As we experience the frustrations of living in a fallen world, we can easily begin to wonder if any story ever has an ending in which everyone truly lives happily ever after.

The good news of the gospel is that the one true story of the world does indeed end with just such a "happily ever after" conclusion for God's people. That rock-solid hope is the foundation upon which Peter and Jude build their repeated exhortations of remaining faithful to Jesus Christ even in the face of threats from false teachers and the difficulties of living in a fallen world.

The Day of the Lord

Both Peter and Jude point their readers to a coming "day" when God will bring judgment on his enemies and salvation for his people. In doing so they are drawing on a deeply rooted Old Testament motif that sheds important light on the message of both 2 Peter and Jude.

The day of the Lord motif emerges most clearly in the prophets. Amos, in what may be the earliest reference to the day of the Lord, rebukes those who long for that day because they think it will be only a day of light and salvation, when in fact it will also bring the darkness and gloom of God's judgment (Amos 5:19–20). Isaiah warns that "the LORD of hosts has a day against all that is proud and lofty, against all that is lifted up—and it shall be brought low. . . . And the haughtiness of man shall be humbled, and the lofty pride of men shall be brought low, and the LORD alone will be exalted in that day" (Isa. 2:12, 17). This day of Yahweh will bring destruction, wrath, and anger upon both rebellious Israel (Isa. 22:1–14) and the nations (Isa. 13:1–22), but redemption for the faithful remnant of his people (Isa. 11:1–16).

Throughout the Old Testament there are a number of different events described as *days of the Lord*, including cataclysmic events such as the destruction of the northern kingdom of Israel (Amos 2:6–16), the destruction of various nations/kingdoms (Jer. 46:10; Obad. 15–18), and the destruction of Jerusalem (Isa. 22:2–25). Often times these days of the Lord are portrayed with cosmic imagery, such as the sun, moon, and stars being darkened and the earth quaking (e.g., Isa. 13:10; Ezek. 32:7–8; Joel 2:10), signaling the end of an era within human history. These individual days of the Lord point to the climactic and final day of the Lord at the end of human history when God will set all things right. Indeed, in some passages it can be difficult to determine whether the day of the Lord in view is a historical event happening in the near future or the final and climactic day of the Lord. An excellent example of this is Zephaniah, who prophesied just a few decades before the Babylonians destroyed Jerusalem and its temple. The judgment oracle begins with Yahweh announcing:

> "I will utterly sweep away everything
>   from the face of the earth," declares the LORD.
> "I will sweep away man and beast;
>   I will sweep away the birds of the heavens
>   and the fish of the sea,
> and the rubble with the wicked.
>   I will cut off mankind
>   from the face of the earth," declares the LORD. (Zeph. 1:2–3)

Yet just a few verses later Zephaniah announces that the day of Yahweh is near, in which he will punish the wickedness of Judah's officials and the idolatry of the people (Zeph. 1:7–14). It will be "A day of wrath . . . , a day of distress and anguish, a day of ruin and devastation, a day of darkness and gloom, a day of clouds and thick darkness" (Zeph. 1:15). Yet just a few verses later, the scene appears to shift again to the end of human history:

> Neither their silver nor their gold
> shall be able to deliver them
> on the day of the wrath of the LORD.
> In the fire of his jealousy,
> all the earth shall be consumed;
> for a full and sudden end
> he will make of all the inhabitants of the earth. (Zeph. 1:18)

Throughout Zephaniah 1 the description of Judah's impending destruction is intertwined with language that appears to describe the final judgment coming on all creation. That is because the day of the Lord when God brings judgment on Jerusalem is a shadow of the great and final day of the Lord when he will do so on all creation.

Joel 2 displays a similar ambiguity when it comes to the day of the Lord. In verses 1–11 the prophet warns that the day of the Lord is near, "a day of darkness and gloom, a day of clouds and thick darkness" (Joel 2:2). That day is "great and very awesome; who can endure it?" (Joel 2:11). As part of the restoration that will come with the day of the Lord, Israel will know that Yahweh is in their midst when he renews the fruitfulness of the land (Joel 2:18–27). The scene then shifts to the future in Joel 2:28–32, where God promises to pour out his Spirit on all flesh, show wonders in the skies above, and save all who call on the name of Yahweh.

This backdrop helps us understand the cosmic imagery that accompanies two significant New Testament events. The first is the crucifixion. The darkness that fell upon the land from the sixth to the ninth hour (i.e., noon until 3 p.m.) and the earthquake that opened the tombs on the morning of Jesus's resurrection signal that the day of the Lord has indeed come (Matt. 27:45–54). The second event is Pentecost. Peter begins his sermon by asserting that the strange phenomena that the crowds are experiencing in connection with the pouring out of the Holy Spirit is the fulfillment God had promised in Joel 2:28–32, which as we saw above includes references to cosmic upheaval. Thus both the crucifixion and Pentecost are yet two more days of the Lord that fall within this sequence that still awaits a culminating and final day of the Lord when all of God's promises will be consummated in a new creation.

But although the crucifixion/resurrection and Pentecost are part of this sequence of days of the Lord, there is a definitive shift in how the New Testament talks about the final and climactic day of the Lord. Because they believed that Jesus Christ was Yahweh in the flesh, the day of the Lord (1 Cor. 5:5; 1 Thess. 5:2; 2 Thess. 2:2) also comes to be referred to as the "day of our Lord Jesus Christ" (1 Cor. 1:8; cf. 2 Cor. 1:14) or simply "the day of Christ" (Phil. 1:6, 10, 2:16).[1] As the focal point of all God's purposes for creation and redemption, it makes sense that the day of the Lord is in fact the day of the Lord Jesus Christ.

It is precisely this dynamic that we see in 2 Peter (and to a lesser degree Jude). In response to scoffers who mock the promise of Christ's return (2 Pet. 3:1–4), Peter reminds his readers that the present heavens and earth "are stored up for fire, being kept until the day of judgment and destruction of the ungodly" (2 Pet. 3:7). The specific mention of that day leads to a more extended discussion of the nature of the day of the Lord. Peter highlights three particular features of that day.

First, God's timetable for the day of the Lord differs from what we might expect (3:8–9). What may from a human perspective appear to be God's slowness in keeping his promise has a greater purpose.[2]

1 See further Richard Bauckham, *2 Peter, Jude*, Word Biblical Themes (Dallas: Word, 1990), 33–34.

2 In addition to the clear allusion to Ps. 90:4 and its surrounding context, there may also be a subtle echo of Hab. 2:3. After instructing the prophet to write down the vision he is giving Habakkuk, Yahweh warns, "For still the vision awaits its appointed time; it hastens to the end—it will not lie. If it seems slow, wait for it; it will surely come; it will

Borrowing language from Psalm 90:4, Peter asserts that "with the Lord one day is as a thousand years, and a thousand years as one day" (2 Pet. 3:8). In its original context, this statement stresses God's eternal nature in contrast to both creation and the span of human life. Despite this short span of life, human beings will be held accountable for their actions, and those who are unrepentant will experience God's wrath (Ps. 90:7–11). As a result, God's people are called to "number our days that we may get a heart of wisdom" as they cry out, "Return, O LORD! How long? Have pity on your servants!" (Ps. 90:12–13). From Psalm 90 Peter draws the conclusion that "the Lord is not slow to fulfill his promise as some count slowness, but is patient toward you, not wishing that any should perish, but that all should reach repentance" (2 Pet. 3:9; cf. Rom. 2:4). What the false teachers see as evidence of a false promise (i.e., the return of Christ) is rather evidence of God's remarkable patience in providing time for people to repent of such foolishness and immoral living. Even within the Old Testament God had made it clear that he is not slow to bring judgment on his enemies (Deut. 7:10) or salvation for his people (Isa. 46:13). What seems like slowness to us from a human perspective is in fact the outworking of God's perfect timing established from before the creation of the world to work all things for his glory.

Second, the day of the Lord will come suddenly (2 Pet. 3:10). Peter asserts that "the day of the Lord will come like a thief" (3:10). He, along with other New Testament authors (1 Thess. 5:2–4; Rev. 3:3; 16:15), borrows this idea directly from Jesus, who while instructing his disciples about his return had compared the unknown hour of his return to the arrival of a thief in the night (Matt. 24:42–44; cf. Luke 12:39). Malachi 3:1 had foretold the sudden and unexpected arrival of the Lord as part of the Old Testament eschatological expectation that Yahweh would bring judgment on his enemies and refinement for his

---

not delay" (Hab. 2:3). As they wait for the fulfillment of this vision, God explains that the "the righteous shall live by his faith" (Hab. 2:4), a text cited several times in the NT (Rom. 1:17; Gal. 3:11; Heb. 10:38) and likely alluded to numerous other times. See further Richard Bauckham, *Jude, 2 Peter*, WBC 50 (Dallas: Word, 1990), 310–11.

people. Whereas the delay of Christ's return leads the false teachers to conclude it will never happen, that same delay could lull God's people into a sense of complacency that leads to immoral living. Even as they await the return of Christ, believers must remain vigilant in their pursuit of godliness to ensure their entrance into the eternal kingdom of our Lord Jesus Christ (2 Pet. 1:2–11).

Third, the day of the Lord will result in the transformation of the cosmos (3:10–14). As we will see below, whether Peter has in view a completely new creation or the complete renewal of the current creation is widely debated. But here it is sufficient to note that Peter envisions the new creation as radically different from the present creation.

By contrast Jude refers explicitly to the day of the Lord only once. Describing the judgment awaiting the angelic beings who rejected God's appointed boundaries, Jude asserts that God "has kept [them] in eternal chains under gloomy darkness until the judgment of the great day" (Jude 6).[3] Yet in the closing benediction—without explicitly using the word *day*—Jude also points his readers to their experience on that climactic day of the Lord (24–25). After affirming that God is able to keep his people from stumbling, Jude states that on that great day God will present his people "blameless before the presence of his glory with great joy" (24). When Solomon dedicated the temple, the cloud of God's glorious presence filled it so that not even the priests could stand in his presence to minister (1 Kings 8:11; cf. Ex. 40:35). Yet on the last day, when God has completed his work of making his people truly blameless, they will be able to stand in his presence with great joy. "Jude here pictures the last day as the eschatological festival of worship, in which the achievement of God's purposes for his people will take the form of his presentation of them as perfect sacrifices in the heavenly sanctuary, offered up to the glory of God amid the jubilation of the worshipers."[4] Only then will God's people be able to experience fully what Psalm 100:2 describes: "Serve the Lord with gladness! Come

3 The expression "great day" may be a shorthand for OT expressions like "great and awesome day of the Lord" (Joel 2:31; Mal. 4:5) or "great day of the Lord" (Zeph. 1:14).

4 Bauckham, *2 Peter, Jude*, 27–28.

into his presence with joyful singing!" (AT).[5] God has promised that the consummation of his creational and redemptive purposes will result in overwhelming joy for his people (Isa. 66:7–14). Because God is able to present his people before him blameless on the last day, "God, our Savior, through Jesus Christ our Lord" is worthy to receive "glory, majesty, dominion, and authority, before all time and now and forever. Amen" (Jude 25). God has been worthy of praise from eternity past and is currently worthy of all praise. But on the great and climactic day of the Lord that awaits God's people in the future, his glory will be manifested in all its radiance to all of creation in celebration of Jesus Christ. And that will be the ultimate source of our great joy.

New Creation as Re-Creation

The culmination of God's promises is dwelling with Christ in a new heavens and a new earth, so it is no surprise that Peter points his readers to this reality in the midst of their struggle to remain true to the gospel in the face of opposition from false teachers: "But according to his promise we are waiting for new heavens and a new earth in which righteousness dwells" (2 Pet. 3:13). Although a number of Old Testament texts point toward this reality, the most prominent are in Isaiah.

The place to begin is Isaiah 65:17–25,[6] where Yahweh announces, "For behold, I create new heavens and a new earth, and the former things shall not be remembered or come into mind" (65:17). Yahweh's joy in Jerusalem and his people will so pervade the new creation that his redeemed people will no longer weep (Isa. 65:18–19). They will experience long life in an abundant land where they enjoy the fruit of their labor (Isa. 65:20–23). Yahweh will be so near to his people that he will respond to their prayers before they even finish speaking them (Isa. 65:24). The hostility embedded within creation itself because of the curse will be gone, and Yahweh will reign from his holy mountain

5 The overlap in wording between Ps. 100:2 [LXX 99:2] and Jude 24 is more obvious in the LXX.

6 Numerous texts within Isaiah refer to this new creation (e.g., 26:6–12; 32:15–20; 43:16–21; 51:3), but they culminate in this description in 65:17–25.

(Isa. 65:25). The prophet returns to this vision at the conclusion of the book in the next chapter (Isa. 66:22–24). The new heavens and new earth will remain before Yahweh forever, as will his redeemed people. All flesh will come to worship Yahweh and acknowledge him as the one true God. Peter's assertion that the new creation will be a place where righteousness dwells also has Isaianic roots. Isaiah 32:16 promises that when God pours out his Spirit on his people, one of the results will be that "righteousness [will] abide in the fruitful field." In the new creation there will be no need for sun or moon because Yahweh himself will be an "everlasting light" (Isa. 60:20), and as a result, "your people shall all be righteous; they shall possess the land forever, the branch of my planting, the work of my hands, that I might be glorified" (Isa. 60:21). While Peter's vision of the new heavens and new earth likely draws from a number of Old Testament texts and motifs, there should be little doubt that it is thoroughly Isaianic.

The promise of a new creation stretches our finite human minds. So it should come as no surprise that the language Peter uses to describe the transition from the current creation to the new creation is not only difficult to understand but open to different interpretations. Perhaps the most challenging question is whether Peter envisions the complete destruction of the current creation and the bringing into existence of the new creation *ex nihilo* (i.e., from nothing) or whether the current creation will be transformed into the new creation through the purging of God's fiery judgment.

The place to begin is with a closer look at the specific language Peter uses in 3:10–13, which states:

> But the day of the Lord will come like a thief, and then the heavens will pass away with a roar, and the heavenly bodies will be burned up and dissolved, and the earth and the works that are done on it will be exposed. Since all these things are thus to be dissolved, what sort of people ought you to be in lives of holiness and godliness, waiting for and hastening the coming of the day of God, because of which the heavens will be set on fire and dissolved, and the heavenly bodies

> will melt as they burn! But according to his promise we are waiting for new heavens and a new earth in which righteousness dwells.

In verse 10 Peter identifies three things that will happen on the day of the Lord. The first is that the heavens will pass away with a roar. The verb rendered "pass away" (*parerchomai*) occurs in connection with heaven and/or earth in the Gospels, where Jesus contrasts the eternal nature of his word with the eventual end of this creation (Matt. 5:18; 24:35; Mark 13:31; Luke 16:17; 21:33).[7] The verb itself has the sense of "to come to an end and so no longer be there."[8] This passing away will happen with a roar, a word that refers to "a rushing sound, whether the whizzing of an arrow, the rush of wings, or the hissing of snakes. In this context we should think of the crackling sound of fire, destroying the heavens."[9] Second, the basic elements of the universe will be destroyed with fire. The word translated "heavenly bodies" (*stoicheion*) more commonly refers to the basic elements of the universe (ESV mg.), which in the ancient world were understood to be earth, air, fire, and water. It is these basic elements of the universe that will be destroyed with intense fire. Third, the earth and the works done on it will be exposed for judgment. Although the specific wording of the Greek text is disputed,[10] Peter's point appears to be that once the current creation is consumed by fire, all that humanity has done will be laid bare before God in judgment. The opening line of 2 Peter 3:11 summarizes these three events on the day of the Lord with the expression "these things are thus to be dissolved," language that again suggests that the complete destruction of the current creation is in view.

Peter uses similar language just a few verses later in 3:12, where he asserts that two things will happen because of the day of God. The first

7 This same verb also appears in a variant reading of Rev. 21:1 to describe the "first heaven and the first earth" passing away.

8 BDAG *parerchomai* (3).

9 Thomas R. Schreiner, *1–2 Peter and Jude*, Christian Standard Commentary (Nashville, TN: B&H, 2020), 459.

10 On the difficulties of the specific wording of the Greek text and its meaning, see the helpful summary discussion in Schreiner, *1–2 Peter and Jude*, 461–64.

is that the heavens will be destroyed with fire, applying language used in verse 10 to describe the fate of the elements now to describe the fiery end of the heavens. The second is that because of this fiery judgment the elements will melt. Peter uses a rare Greek word that in the LXX describes the defeat and judgment of God's enemies.[11] Peter may borrow language and imagery from several texts in Isaiah. In describing the day of Yahweh, Isaiah 24:23 (LXX) notes that "then the brick will be dissolved, and the wall will fall, because the Lord will reign in Sion and in Jerusalem, and before the elders he will be glorified" (NETS). Isaiah 34:4 (LXX) asserts that when judgment comes upon the nations, "all the powers of the heavens will melt."[12] Isaiah 63:19–64:1 had warned that when the Lord would appear in judgment the mountains "would melt as wax melts from the fire" (NETS).

Thus while acknowledging the obvious metaphorical use of language to describe an event that is beyond our ability to comprehend, the most natural and straightforward reading of this passage seems to favor the complete destruction of the current creation. Yet other passages of Scripture and theological considerations—both within 1–2 Peter and from the rest of Scripture—may suggest the opposite conclusion, that the new creation is a renewal of the existing creation.

First, Peter clearly sees the flood as a type of the judgment, de-creation, and re-creation that awaits the present universe (2 Pet. 3:5–7). He draws a contrast between the preflood world ("the world that then existed," 3:6) and the postflood world ("the heavens and earth that now exist," 3:7). This present postflood world is "stored up for fire, being kept until the day of judgment and destruction of the ungodly" (3:7). The inference seems to be that just as the judgment measured out through the flood did not result in the complete destruction of the preflood world but rather a transformation of it, so too in the final judgment

11 Ex. 15:15; Isa. 24:23; 34:4; 64:1; Mic. 1:4; Nah. 1:6; Hab. 3:6; Zech. 14:12. This Greek verb (*tēkō*) occurs nowhere else in the NT. The destruction of the universe by fire is described in several Second Temple Jewish texts (e.g., *1 En.* 1:6; 97:2; *T. Levi* 4:1).

12 Following Schreiner, *1–2 Peter and Jude*, 468, who bases this on the reading of the LXX in Vaticanus and Lucian.

through fire, the present world will not be completely destroyed but transformed. But although it is true that the flood is a type of the final judgment that awaits the current creation, there are important differences. The first is that God used water rather than fire. Second, and more importantly, the renewal of the present creation that took place through the flood did not eliminate the presence and effects of sin, death, and the curse. Perhaps this distinction suggests that whereas the renewal of creation through the flood was adequate for God's purposes for that point in redemptive history, the complete elimination of sin, death, and the curse requires the destruction of the present creation and the creation of a completely new heavens and earth.

Second, other passages of Scripture seem to indicate the redemption of the present creation rather than its complete destruction. Perhaps most noteworthy is Romans 8:18–25, where Paul personifies creation as waiting "with eager longing for the revealing of the sons of God" (Rom. 8:19). The reason for this eager longing is that creation was subjected to futility (i.e., the curse) when Adam rebelled against God (Rom. 8:20). God did this "in hope that the creation itself will be set free from its bondage to corruption and obtain the freedom of the glory of the children of God" (Rom. 8:20–21). As a result creation itself groans with pains of childbirth in anticipation of being freed from its corruption by sin, death, and the curse (Rom. 8:22). The most straightforward reading of this passage points toward the transformation of the present creation, not its replacement.

Further complicating the issue is that in Revelation 21:1–8 there is language that could easily support either transformation and renewal or destruction and replacement. The fact that John sees the first heaven and the first earth pass away and the new Jerusalem "coming down out of heaven" seems to suggest replacement (Rev. 21:1–2). Yet after this description God announces, "I am making all things new" (Rev. 21:5), language that seems to suggest transformation. This ambiguity is further reflected in Isaiah. While some passages describing the new creation use the same Hebrew verb (*bārāʾ*) found in Genesis 1:1 to describe God's initial act of creation *ex nihilo* (Isa. 41:20; 65:17–18), other texts use the more generic verb *make* (ʿāśâ) instead (Isa. 41:20; 43:19; 66:22).

At the end of the day, it is difficult to be definitive as to whether Peter envisions the destruction of the present creation and its replacement with a new creation made *ex nihilo*, or whether his language—albeit vivid—is a metaphorical way of describing the renewal and transformation of the present creation. Regardless of what one concludes, we must not lose sight of what is clear. Our hope rests in the promise of a "new heavens and a new earth in which righteousness dwells" (2 Pet. 3:13). And that hope compels us to live a certain way in the present.

Living in Light of That Day

Rightly understood, eschatology leads to ethics. Because God's people understand God's plan to culminate human history in a new creation, they are called to live in certain ways. God is far less interested in satisfying our curiosity about the details of how human history ends than he is about exhorting us to live in a way that will prepare us for the end of human history.

The New Testament authors were not innovative in making this connection. In the broadest sense, this relationship between eschatology and ethics is embedded in Genesis 1–2. God commissioned humanity to "be fruitful and multiply and fill the earth and subdue it, and have dominion over the fish of the sea and over the birds of the heavens and over every living thing that moves on the earth" (Gen. 1:28). That commission establishes the eschatological goal—God's image bearers ruling over creation as an extension of his own rule. In light of this goal, God instructs humanity to live in a certain way—prohibiting them from eating from the tree of the knowledge of good and evil (Gen. 2:16–17).

The same is true of God's commission to Israel at Mount Sinai. With Israel gathered together, Yahweh announces, "Now therefore, if you will indeed obey my voice and keep my covenant, you shall be my treasured possession among all peoples, for all the earth is mine; and you shall be to me a kingdom of priests and a holy nation"

(Ex. 19:5–6).[13] In the chapters that follow, God gives the law to his people to instruct them how to live as God's people in anticipation of inheriting the land where they will live as a kingdom of priests and a holy nation. Forty years later as a new generation of Israelites prepares to actually enter the land, Deuteronomy recounts God, through Moses, restating his law to the people so they will know how to live in light of God fulfilling his promises.

The Old Testament prophets continued in this vein of rooting ethics in eschatology as they regularly called God's people to live lives of righteousness in anticipation of God fulfilling his promises of judgment and salvation. Isaiah 2:2–4 lays out a compelling vision of the latter days, in which the nations will stream to the mountain of God to worship Yahweh and learn his ways. In response to this eschatological promise, Isaiah writes, "O house of Jacob, come, let us walk in the light of the Lord" (Isa. 2:5). In Jeremiah 29 the prophet writes to the exiles living in Babylon, instructing them to prepare for a lengthy stay in exile. They should remain faithful to Yahweh and seek the welfare of the city where they live (Jer. 29:1–9). These exhortations are rooted in the promise that Yahweh will one day restore them from exile and bring them back to the land (Jer. 29:10–14).

These Old Testament precedents set the pattern for both Peter and Jude. After the initial greeting, 2 Peter begins with a reminder that God has given his people everything necessary for life and godliness through his precious promises (2 Pet. 1:3–4). Based on that foundation, Peter calls believers to pursue growth in a series of character qualities (1:5–7). Growth in these character qualities will ensure fruitfulness and confirm one's calling and election (1:8–10). It is by practicing these qualities that "there will be richly provided for you an entrance into the eternal kingdom of our Lord and Savior Jesus Christ" (1:11). The call to pursue character qualities in the present is grounded in being able to enter Christ's kingdom on the last day.

13 Israel's commission is a modified version of Adam's commission; see further Benjamin L. Gladd, *From Adam and Israel to the Church: A Biblical Theology of the People of God* (Downers Grove, IL: IVP Academic, 2019), 35–57.

Peter continues to link ethics and eschatology in the following chapter. The four Old Testament examples in 2:4–10 reinforce this connection. On the negative side, the angels who sinned (2:4), the world of the ungodly in the days of the flood (2:5), the cities of Sodom and Gomorrah (2:6), and the wicked who lived around Lot (2:7–8) all serve as examples of the unrighteous who, because they did not rightly grasp the reality of final judgment, rejected God's appointed boundaries and faced condemnation. Positively, Noah (2:5) and Lot (2:7) are examples of those who by contrast are righteous and will therefore be rescued on the last day (2:9–10). It is this larger Old Testament pattern that establishes the framework for Peter's condemnation of the false teachers. Their rejection of final judgment before the Lord leads to their indulgence in sexual immorality (2:10, 14, 18), arrogance (2:11–12, 18), and greed (2:15–16).

By contrast, a right understanding of eschatology leads to a life shaped by God's promise of a new creation (3:11–18). Because we know that the present creation will be dissolved, our lives as believers should be characterized by three things (3:11–12). The first is holiness, which refers to living a morally pure life set apart for God's purposes (cf. 1 Pet. 1:14–16). Second is godliness, a term that denotes living with a Godward orientation in every aspect of life. Finally, we should be characterized by "waiting for and hastening the coming of the day of God" (2 Pet. 3:12). Biblically speaking, waiting is not passive but rather an eager anticipation that produces action (cf. Rom. 8:19–23). Hastening likely has in view the Jewish belief that God hastens the end in connection with his people's repentance (cf. 2 Pet. 3:9), though Peter may also have in view our godly lives, prayers (Matt. 6:10), and evangelistic efforts (Matt. 24:14). This does not preclude God's sovereignty, since he accomplishes his purposes through the actions of his people. Peter returns to this theme of waiting in 2 Peter 3:13, where he notes that the new creation believers hope for is a place "in which righteousness dwells." Those who hope for a new creation where righteousness dwells are motivated to live lives of righteousness in the present. Put another way, those who eagerly await the new creation diligently pursue lives that are "without spot or blemish, and at peace" (3:14). Our eschatological hope motivates us to regard God's patience as salvation (3:15), reject false teaching that destabilizes our faith (3:17), and "grow in the grace and knowledge of our Lord and Savior Jesus Christ" (3:18).

Similar dynamics are present in Jude as well. Like Peter, Jude uses Old Testament examples of those who rebelled against God's authority as a warning of the final judgment that is coming upon all who pursue the path trod by the false teachers (Jude 5–16). The apostles had warned that in the last days there would be scoffers who would pursue ungodly desires and cause division (17–19). In contrast to such scoffers, believers should pursue spiritual growth as they are "waiting for the mercy of our Lord Jesus Christ that leads to eternal life" (20–21). Jude's well-known benediction also connects eschatological hope with a certain way of life in the present (24–25). Because God is able to keep his people from stumbling and present them blameless in his presence with great joy, believers are motivated to keep themselves in the love of God (21).

Conclusion

Life in this fallen world can be difficult. Fighting against our own sinful tendencies and experiencing the effects of the curse in this broken world can easily lead to discouragement. But knowing that God has promised a new creation for us where he will dwell with us forever provides the encouragement to remain faithful to Jesus no matter what. It also provides us with the motivation to pursue lives of godliness as we wait the day when we will appear before the Lord blameless with great joy. Knowing the happy ending of God's story enables us to embrace even suffering on the way to that glorious destination.

Conclusion

IN THE MIDST OF A WORLD that often seems out of control, knowing our ultimate destiny is a source of great comfort and motivation to press on in the face of serious challenges and opposition to the gospel. Jude and Peter both knew that in order for Christians to live faithfully as God's people, they need to look both backward and forward—backward to what God has done throughout redemptive history, and forward to what God has promised to do in the future. Both these realities are found in God's word, consisting of "the predictions of the holy prophets [i.e., the Old Testament] and the commandment of the Lord and Savior through your apostles [i.e., the New Testament]" (2 Pet. 3:2). In it we find "the faith that was once for all delivered to the saints" (Jude 3). This word is the result of men speaking "from God as they were carried along by the Holy Spirit" (2 Pet. 1:21). As a result, it is sufficient for everything pertaining to life and godliness (1:3–5).

The God who speaks in this word is the triune God—Father, Son, and Holy Spirit (Jude 20–21). Each person of the Trinity works in cooperation to accomplish the redemption of God's people. Peter and Jude put the Son on center stage in redemptive history, stressing his authority as Lord and Master (2 Pet. 2:4; Jude 4). He is not just the Savior of his people (2 Pet. 1:1, 11; 2:20; 3:2, 18), but he is also the one who will render final judgment on all God's enemies (2:4–10; 3:4–13; Jude 5–15).

Given the priority and importance of God's word, it is no surprise that false teachers attack it. Throughout redemptive history they have followed a pattern first used in the garden by Satan himself. They begin by questioning God's word, subtly seeking to undermine one's confidence in what God has said (2 Pet. 3:16; Jude 4). From there they move on to directly contradicting God's word, arguing that God cannot be trusted to tell us the truth and nothing but the truth (2 Pet. 3:4; Jude 6–18). With the truth of God's word now discarded, false teachers offer what they claim is a better alternative that appeals to our natural appetites (2 Pet. 2:2–22). Examples of this pattern are seen throughout redemptive history, such as Balaam, Cain, and Korah (2:15–16; Jude 11). Knowing the true gospel allows believers to not only resist the enticement of false teachers but also rescue those ensnared by it (2 Pet. 1:12–15; Jude 3, 22–23).

Despite the very real threat posed by false teachers and the challenges of life in a fallen world, believers can rest in the knowledge that the God who saved them is the God who also keeps them. Believers are kept by Jesus Christ (Jude 1), who is able to "keep you from stumbling and to present you blameless before the presence of his glory with great joy" (24). Even though believers live in a world where immorality is pervasive, God is able to "rescue the godly from trials, and to keep the unrighteous under punishment until the day of judgment" (2 Pet. 2:9). God preserves his people by empowering them to persevere in the true faith until the end. Believers keep themselves in God's love by pursuing a growing faith, praying in the Spirit, and waiting for the mercy of Jesus at his return (Jude 20–21). They can confirm their calling and election by pursuing growth in various character qualities and thus ensure entrance into Christ's eternal kingdom (2 Pet. 1:3–11).

That eternal kingdom is further described as a new heavens and a new earth, the final destination of God's people. The day of the Lord promised in the Old Testament will bring an even greater judgment on creation than the flood (3:4–7). God is not slow about keeping his promise; the seeming delay in God consummating his promises is to give more time for sinners to repent (3:8–10). When the day of the Lord finally does come like a thief in the night (3:10), it will result in either the complete destruction or the complete transformation of the present creation (3:10–12). The new heavens and new earth will be a place where righteousness dwells because Jesus the righteous one dwells there with his righteous people (3:13). That hope of a new creation motivates believers to live "lives of holiness and godliness, waiting for and hastening the coming of the day of God" (3:11–12).

Although 2 Peter and Jude were written nearly two thousand years ago, their message remains relevant for our contemporary moment. So it seems only appropriate that we end with closing benedictions from these letters as a means of God speaking his blessing over us:

> But grow in the grace and knowledge of our Lord and Savior Jesus Christ. To him be the glory both now and to the day of eternity. Amen. (2 Pet. 3:18)

> Now to him who is able to keep you from stumbling and to present you blameless before the presence of his glory with great joy, to the only God, our Savior, through Jesus Christ our Lord, be glory, majesty, dominion, and authority, before all time and now and forever. Amen. (Jude 24–25)

Bibliography

Barclay, John. "Mirror-Reading a Polemical Letter: Galatians as a Test Case." *Journal for the Study of the New Testament* 31 (1987): 73–93.

Bateman IV, Herbert W. *Jude*. Evangelical Exegetical Commentary. Bellingham, WA: Lexham Press, 2017.

Bauckham, Richard. *Jude and the Relatives of Jesus in the Early Church*. T&T Clark Academic Paperbacks. London: T&T Clark, 2004.

———. *Jude, 2 Peter*. Word Biblical Commentary. Dallas: Word, 1990.

———. *2 Peter, Jude*. Word Biblical Themes. Dallas: Word, 1990.

Beckwith, Roger T. *The Old Testament Canon of the New Testament Church and Its Background in Early Judaism*. Grand Rapids, MI: Eerdmans, 1986.

Carson, D. A. *The Enduring Authority of the Christian Scriptures*. Grand Rapids, MI: Eerdmans, 2016.

———. "Mirror-Reading with Paul and against Paul: Galatians 2:11–14 as a Test Case." In *Studies in the Pauline Epistles: Essays in Honor of Douglas J. Moo*, edited by Matthew S. Harmon and Jay E. Smith, 99–112. Grand Rapids, MI: Zondervan, 2014.

Crowe, Brandon D. *The Message of the General Epistles in the History of Redemption: Wisdom from James, Peter, John, and Jude*. Phillipsburg, NJ: P&R, 2015.

Davids, Peter H. *The Letters of 2 Peter and Jude*. Pillar New Testament Commentary. Grand Rapids, MI: Eerdmans, 2006.

———. *A Theology of James, Peter, and Jude*. Biblical Theology of the New Testament. Grand Rapids, MI: Zondervan, 2014.

Dean, Kenda Creasy. *Almost Christian: What the Faith of Our Teenagers Is Telling the American Church*. Oxford, UK: Oxford University Press, 2010.

Dempster, Stephen. "The Old Testament Canon, Josephus, and Cognitive Framework." In *The Enduring Authority of the Christian Scriptures*, edited by D. A. Carson, 321–61. Grand Rapids, MI: Eerdmans, 2016.

Ehrman, Bart D. *Lost Christianities: The Battles for Scripture and the Faiths We Never Knew*. New York: Oxford University Press, 2003.

Ellis, E. Earle. *The Old Testament in Early Christianity: Canon and Interpretation in the Light of Modern Research*. Grand Rapids, MI: Baker, 1992.

Gladd, Benjamin L. *From Adam and Israel to the Church: A Biblical Theology of the People of God*. Essential Studies in Biblical Theology. Downers Grove, IL: IVP Academic, 2019.

Green, Gene L. *Jude and 2 Peter*. Baker Exegetical Commentary on the New Testament. Grand Rapids, MI: Baker Academic, 2008.

Gupta, N. K. "Mirror-Reading Moral Issues in Paul's Letters." *Journal for the Study of the New Testament* 34, no. 4 (2012): 361–81.

Gurtner, Daniel M. *Introducing the Pseudepigrapha of Second Temple Judaism: Message, Context, and Significance*. Grand Rapids, MI: Baker Academic, 2020.

Hamilton, James M. *What Is Biblical Theology? A Guide to the Bible's Story, Symbolism, and Patterns*. Wheaton, IL: Crossway, 2014.

Harmon, Matthew S. "2 Peter." In *Hebrews–Revelation*, edited by Iain M. Duguid, James M. Hamilton, and Jay Sklar, 363–410. Vol. 12 of ESV Expository Commentary. Wheaton, IL: Crossway, 2018.

———. "Jude." In *Hebrews–Revelation*, edited by Iain M. Duguid, James M. Hamilton, and Jay Sklar, 501–23. Vol. 12 of ESV Expository Commentary. Wheaton, IL: Crossway, 2018.

Keller, Timothy J. *Counterfeit Gods: The Empty Promises of Money, Sex, and Power, and the Only Hope That Matters*. New York: Dutton, 2009.

Kline, Meredith G. *The Structure of Biblical Authority*. 2nd ed. Eugene, OR: Wipf & Stock, 1989.

Köstenberger, Andreas J., and Michael J. Kruger. *The Heresy of Orthodoxy: How Contemporary Culture's Fascination with Diversity Has Reshaped Our Understanding of Early Christianity*. Wheaton, IL: Crossway, 2010.

Kruger, Michael J. *The Question of Canon: Challenging the Status Quo in the New Testament Debate*. Downers Grove, IL: InterVarsity Press, 2013.

Malone, Andrew S. *God's Mediators: A Biblical Theology of Priesthood*. New Studies in Biblical Theology. Downers Grove, IL: InterVarsity Press, 2017.

Moo, Douglas J. *2 Peter, Jude: From Biblical Text to Contemporary Life*. NIV Application Commentary. Grand Rapids, MI: Zondervan, 1996.

Schreiner, Thomas R. *1–2 Peter and Jude*. Christian Standard Commentary. Nashville, TN: B&H, 2020.

Silva, Moisés. *Interpreting Galatians: Explorations in Exegetical Method*. 2nd ed. Grand Rapids, MI: Baker, 2001.

Smith, Christian, and Melinda Lundquist Denton. *Soul Searching: The Religious and Spiritual Lives of American Teenagers*. Oxford, UK: Oxford University Press, 2005.

Thurén, Lauri. "Hey Jude! Asking for the Original Situation and Message of a Catholic Epistle." *New Testament Studies* 43, no. 3 (1997): 451–65.

Tozer, A. W. *The Knowledge of the Holy*. 1st HarperCollins gift ed. New York: HarperSanFrancisco, 1992.

Wasserman, Tommy. *The Epistle of Jude: Its Text and Transmission*. Coniectanea Biblica. New Testament. Stockholm, SE: Almqvist & Wiksell International, 2006.

General Index

Scripture Index

New Testament Theology

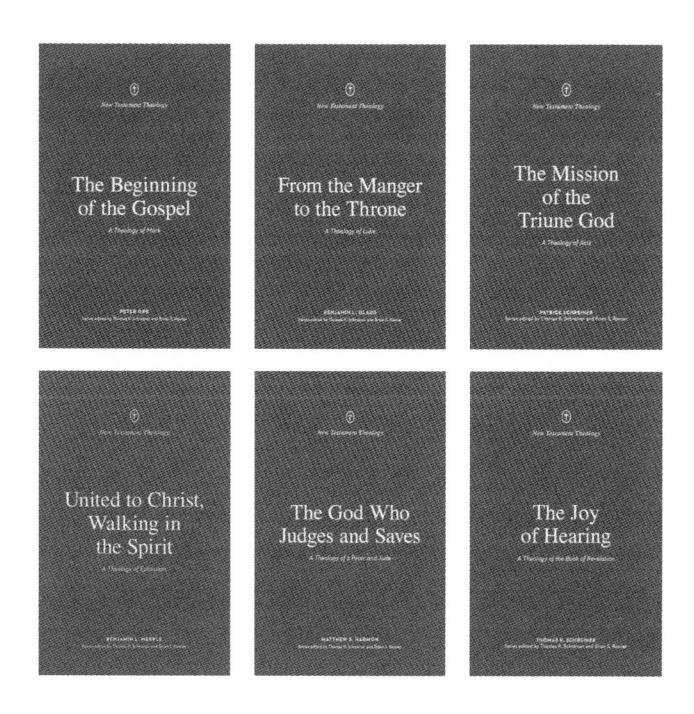

Edited by Thomas R. Schreiner and Brian S. Rosner, this series presents clear, scholarly overviews of the main theological themes of each book of the New Testament, examining what they reveal about God and his relation to the world in the context of the overarching biblical narrative.

For more information, visit **crossway.org**.